DEDICATION

To H.P. for making it all possible

ACKNOWLEDGMENTS

Writing is only part of bringing a book into the world. A publisher who "gets it," contributors, editors, artists, printers, and office and warehouse people all did their part to bring this book into being and into your hands. It's this whole crew I want to thank for their special skills and contributions. My very special thanks go out to:

My publisher, Judy Galbraith, for her continual support and her willingness to share her commitment to the young people she serves. The hope that the system will someday change to allow for the full development of human potential is kept alive in people like her.

My editor, Pamela Espeland, for her patience, sense of humor, and wizardly skills.

The kids who took a risk to share of themselves so intimately and freely.

All of my family and friends, my safety net, who remained available, supportive, and patient with me throughout the writing of this book.

Picole, for her presence and patience as I worked on my dream.

CONTENTS

INTRODUCTION

Which of these statements sound as if you might have said them or thought them in the past few days, weeks, or months?

- I feel bored in school.
- Sometimes my life is overwhelming (getting up early all the time, too much homework, fighting with my brother [sister], feeling left out, arguments with parents, problems with my friends and their friends, and _____).
- I wish I was (smarter, friendlier, more popular, athletic, _____).
- I think I'm getting sick.
- I'm afraid of failing.
- Too many people expect too much from me.
- I can't do everything I'm supposed to do.
- I'm not happy with myself or what I'm doing.
- I want to sleep for a long time.

If some or even most of these statements sound familiar to you, you're not alone. Hundreds of young people have told me that they feel overwhelmed, frustrated, inadequate, tired, or *stressed out* by the challenges in their lives.

You'd think that life would be less complicated when you're young. You'd think that you could just enjoy yourself and have fun. But being a teenager today means having a life that is often full of stress. Few young people get by without paying some emotional or physical price.

Here is how some young people describe the way they experience stress:

- "Emotionally confused, mentally exhausted, and physically hyper."
- "Tired, drained, fat, ugly, pushed around by others."
- "Back pains, can't sleep, listless, depressed."
- "I get headaches. I feel like I am in a tightly closed box."
- "Shaky, wanting to get away, helpless."
- "A complete failure."
- "Frustrated, worn out, sick, angry."
- "Down, mad, stupid, alone, nothing."
- "All crumpled up."
- "Scared and alone."
- "Rejected, sad, unpopular, ugly, stupid."
- "Trapped and demented."
- "Like I need something to eat all the time."
- "Grouchy, moody, bored with life."
- "I feel like crying."
- "I feel like screaming."
- "I feel like I'm going to break."

WHAT IS STRESS?

So what exactly is this problem called stress? Why do so many people have trouble with it? And why is it so hard to manage?

Stress is the *general* feeling you get as a result of a lot of different kinds of problems and challenges. Imagine that every worry, relationship problem, tough homework assignment, and issue with a parent is a separate rubber band around your head. As your life gets more complicated, more rubber bands are layered on until your head is completely covered. Stress is the pressure you feel on the inside.

Human beings have limits to the amount of internal pressure they can stand. When you're close to your limit, life can feel depressing, overwhelming, frightening, even dangerous.

It's hard to do something about your stress when there are so many rubber bands that you can't tell which *one* is making you feel bad. Instead, you have an overall sense that something is wrong. You may feel anxious, but you can't name the problem that is causing or contributing to your anxiety. It's almost impossible to know where to start fixing things when you're dealing with a general feeling.

INVISIBLE TIGERS

This book is called *Fighting Invisible Tigers* because when your life is very stressful, it can feel like you're in a thick jungle with lots of dangerous tigers—ferocious, hungry, invisible tigers. You can't see them, but you can sense them quietly stalking you. Imagine...

You're alone in a steamy, spooky jungle. You've been hacking through it for days while huge mosquitoes chomp at your flesh. Weird noises and strange smells fill the air, and the heat is enough to fry your brain. And every now and then you hear a deep, menacing growl....

Now imagine what it would be like to live with this fear every day—always watchful, on edge, and ready to react. Being on guard every minute takes an enormous amount of energy. A person with many tigers and no way to manage them can get pushed to the limit in a hurry.

What if you had to live in the jungle for years and years? When high levels of stress continue over long periods of time, this can lead to illness, depression, and other big problems. Chronic stress is serious business.

THE BAD NEWS

- You can't cure stress by thinking about it or worrying about it.

- Being smart, creative, motivated, or energetic does not necessarily help relieve stress and can even add to the stress in your life.

- There are no easy answers or quick fixes for managing stress.

- There are only a few places—some schools, religious organizations, boys' and girls' clubs, after-care programs, and families—that teach teenagers the long-term lifeskills they need to successfully deal with stress. But most young people get little or no guidance when it comes to managing stress.

So what can you do to keep from being wounded or gobbled up as you journey through the jungle of life?

THE GOOD NEWS

- You can learn about stress and understand why you sometimes feel oppressed, depressed, overwhelmed, or exhausted.

- You can learn to better understand the complex emotions and physical responses that all people experience when they are under pressure.

- You can develop an "early warning system" to help you know when to do something about the increasing stress in your life.

- You can learn positive ways to take care of yourself during the hard times.

- You can learn new skills to gain more control over your life and to manage your tigers.

- You can learn to create a life in which the tigers can't eat away at the fun and generally positive attitude you should be experiencing every day.

- You can start here and now.

> **"The illiterate of the future are not those who can't read or write, but those who can't learn, unlearn and relearn."**
> Alvin Toffler

ABOUT THIS BOOK

Fighting Invisible Tigers is more than a survival guide to life under demanding conditions. It's a mini-course in becoming the best person you can be, written with help from hundreds of young people like you.

Part I, "Life in the Jungle," helps you to:

- understand your physical and emotional responses to stress
- learn about some common misconceptions young people have about handling stress that guarantee trouble
- identify healthy and unhealthy ways of dealing with stress
- recognize the important difference between coping with stress and managing stress.

Part II, "Self-Care for Tiger Bites," teaches you how to:

- know when you've reached your limit
- avoid being your own worst stressor
- take care of yourself physically and emotionally
- stay in touch with what's right when it feels as if everything's wrong
- get help from people you trust.

Part III, "Lifeskills," introduces you to skills that will help you to:

- have more control over your life
- develop a definition of success that works for you
- feel more confident and boost your self-esteem
- make and keep good friends
- express anger and other feelings in positive ways
- develop a program for getting physically healthy
- understand how to use play and humor for stress resistance and relief

■ find a balance among all the things that make up a successful life.

Naturally, none of this will happen just because you read a
book. But by reading this book, you'll gain a better understanding
of what is possible for you, and you'll learn how to get started.

The *goals* of this book are to help you know more about the
experience of stress, give you some tips on taking care of yourself
during the hard times, and offer you some tools you can use to
create a great life for yourself over the long term.

My *hope* is that you'll eventually become a more resilient,
stress-resistant person. Someone who is well-equipped for the
adventure of life. Someone whose potential isn't blocked by the
fear and hopelessness of too much stress, but whose heart and
mind are open to the joys and satisfactions available on the
journey.

No matter how you feel about yourself right now, you have
options. You can make self-respecting choices. And you deserve
to know how to manage the challenges in your life. That's what
this book is about.

Good luck, and my very best wishes go with you.

Earl Hipp

PART 1

LIFE IN THE

JUNGLE

FIGHTING INVISIBLE TIGERS

You may think that stress is a modern phenomenon, but that's only because there's been so much talk about it in recent years. Actually, it was around as long ago as four million B.C., when our cave-dwelling ancestors were struggling to survive. Even then, there were problems that made life complicated, difficult, and scary—fires that wouldn't start, spoiled meat, damp caves, and the lack of enough warm fur pelts to wear. But worst of all were the animals that saw our forerunners as food.

THE FIGHT-OR-FLIGHT RESPONSE

On a nice day in the jungle, for example, a huge sabertooth tiger with lunch on its mind could leap out in front of these poor people. Because most hungry tigers are in no mood for conversation, smart cave dwellers learned to react right away and either bash the cat or dash for safety. This required a finely tuned nervous system that could instantly mobilize the body into what we

now call the "fight-or-flight" response. Prehistoric folks who weren't good at it became tasty snacks, and those who could run or fight lived to tell the story around the fire. Over millions of years, the people with the best fight-or-flight skills survived, and the others...let's just say that they didn't come home after lunch.

The process of natural selection means that you have inherited an incredible nervous system. It gets your body ready to do battle or run like the wind at the first hint of danger. It is so sensitive that even thinking about tigers and other frightening things can be enough to get you all fired up.

While most of us never have to face real tigers, the world you live in can feel every bit as threatening as the one your long-ago ancestors experienced. For example, it can be anxiety-producing to:

- watch your parents have a major fight
- take a test in a tough class
- move away from friends, or have friends move away
- know that some students bring weapons to school

- worry about getting into a fight
- see a friend get drunk or high
- think about life after school
- think about world hunger, pollution, or the national debt.

The problem is, whenever you're up against something that makes you feel threatened, your body still responds as if it's meeting a hungry tiger. At the first hint of danger, off goes the alarm, and instantly you're ready to physically and emotionally fight or flee.

During times of high stress, many different physical events occur inside your body at the same time. If you don't understand what's happening to you, it can feel as if your body is having problems instead of naturally gearing up to deal with the challenges you're facing. As you learn about stress and the changes it creates in your body, you start to recognize these changes as an early-warning system, a set of signals indicating the need to do something about your life in that particular moment.

Here's a description of some of the physical changes that take place in *healthy* bodies during the fight-or-flight response, along with reasons why they happen. While each person's body will react slightly differently, we all experience some version of these events, instantly and automatically, whenever we perceive that we are in danger.

- **Your heart pounds.** The body needs all of the oxygen-rich blood it can get, and it needs it in a hurry, so the heart beats harder and faster.

- **Your hands and feet feel cooler than usual.** The capillaries in your hands and feet constrict to make more blood available at the center of the body and in the large muscles needed for running and fighting.

- **You may feel warm in the face, your cheeks and ears may get pink, and/or you may suddenly develop a "pressure" headache.** The carotid arteries in the neck open up to allow more blood to the brain.

■ **Your mouth may get dry and/or you may have an upset stomach.** The digestive tract shuts down to let its blood be used elsewhere.

■ **You may get "butterflies" in your stomach and/or feel "restless."** Glands and organs produce chemicals that help the body to prepare for running or fighting. The most common of these is adrenaline.

■ **You sweat. Your hands may get clammy.** Anticipating the extra heat that running and fighting generate, the body turns on its climate-control system by producing excess moisture on the surface of the skin. Evaporation of this moisture creates a cooling effect.

It's important to know that it's *perfectly normal* to feel weird physical sensations during times of major stress. Your body isn't malfunctioning. It's working exactly as it should. The question to ask yourself isn't "What's wrong with me?" but "What's happening that is making me feel this way?"

> **"Virtually every organ and every chemical constituent of the human body is involved in the general stress reaction."**
> Dr. Hans Selye, *The Stress of Life*

SHORT-TERM STRESS

The fight-or-flight response takes a lot out of you. Battling real or even invisible tigers is a total body experience. Fortunately, these moments don't last very long. After the danger passes, there is a period during which your body can calm down, rest, and return to normal.

Here's a picture of the typical *short-term stress* pattern:

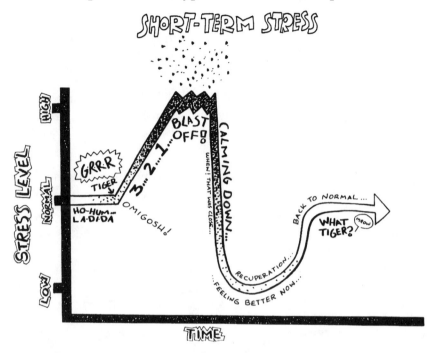

LONG-TERM STRESS

What happens when you live with stress constantly? When your life is full of tigers that never go away? You gradually adapt to higher and higher stress levels, and you may never find the time to calm down, rest, and recuperate. Soon you're living with an *unhealthy* amount of stress and calling it normal. Long-term stress can be dangerous because you may not be aware of the physical and emotional toll it is taking on you.

Why is long-term stress such a problem for so many people?

■ We aren't taught about stress, so we don't recognize it even when we are up to our eyeballs in it.

■ We all have stressors in our lives that we're powerless to do anything about (parental decisions, school rules, homework, problems with friends, feeling unsafe).

■ We face so many challenges that it isn't practical or possible to rest after each one.

■ We're the products of a driven culture. We're taught from an early age that it's good to compete, win, stay busy, and always be productive.

■ Most of us don't know how to relax. Relaxation skills aren't valued by our culture. It's more common (and accepted) to hurry and always do too much than it is to relax and be quiet for a period of time.

■ Even our attempts at play can be filled with competition and pressures to be great at everything we do. Recreation is supposed to be *re-creation*—a chance to renew ourselves. Instead, it turns into *wreckreation*. We end up feeling more strung out and wrung out than when we started.

We all do our best to live in our world full of tigers. We try to be responsible and handle everything that comes our way. Here are some of the things young people do in an effort to keep up and "keep it all together":

- "I skip meals."
- "I sleep less."
- "I try to spend more time helping my family."
- "I cut out my play time."
- "I *never* tell people how I'm feeling."
- "I go it alone and tough it out."
- "I make time."

When you try harder to keep up as the stress in your life increases, you may forget to take time for rest and recuperation. Without realizing it, you gradually lose your energy, positive attitude, and performance edge. Like a woodcutter who never takes time to sharpen the ax, you discover that it's more difficult to do things that used to be easy. Eventually you reach the limit of what you can handle.

**"The trouble with the rat race is that
even if you win, you're still a rat."**
Lily Tomlin

HOW TO TELL WHEN YOU'RE REACHING YOUR LIMIT

There will be times in your life when there are more tigers around than you have the skills to manage—especially since most of us aren't taught *any* skills in tiger management. During those moments, you may experience the symptoms of overload. Here are some of the symptoms young people have reported:

- more trouble with teachers
- needing a lot of sleep or not sleeping well
- wanting to eat all the time or never eating
- headaches, stomach aches, colds, infections, sore muscles
- escapist behavior—overdoing one thing (TV, music, studying, sleeping) and ignoring other things
- withdrawing from friends and family ("Just leave me *alone!*")
- crying for no apparent reason
- feeling like an idiot
- restlessness, anxiety, worrying all the time
- feeling like everything is out of control ("like *I'm* out of control")
- depression, sadness, crabbiness, the blahs.

You may be too busy adapting and coping with your stressors to notice how you are changing. Unconsciously, you keep modifying your definition of what constitutes an acceptable level of stress. Suddenly the symptoms of overload seem to come out of nowhere. One minute you think you're fine, and the next you find yourself doubling over with cramps, tossing and turning at night, yelling at your mom, having two-day headaches, biting your nails, or gobbling whole crates of chips.

On the next page is a picture of a *long-term stress* pattern.

It's frightening and dangerous to live at the limit of your ability to cope. That's why it's important to learn how to deal with stress. But first, let's find out how *not* to deal with it. People have developed an amazing number of beliefs and actions for dealing with stress that are not at all helpful. I call them Tropical Illusions.

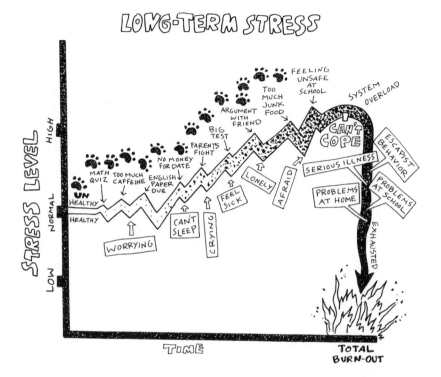

LONG-TERM STRESS

....

READ MORE ABOUT IT

If you want to know more about the physiology of stress, read:

Everything You Need to Know about Stress by Eleanor H. Ayer (New York: Rosen Publishing Group, 1994).

Kicking Your Stress Habits by Donald A. Tubesing (New York: New American Library, 1982).

The Stress of Life by Hans Selye (New York: McGraw Hill, 1978).

Stress without Distress by Hans Selye (New York: Dutton, 1975).

....

TROPICAL ILLUSIONS

There is no stress in the world.

Repeat: There is no stress in the world.

Surprised? Think about it. Where would you go looking for it if you wanted to find stress? The Gobi Desert? South Wales? Chengtu, China?

Stress is something that happens *inside* of people—inside of *you.* It's the result of how you perceive and interpret the challenges you face. To understand this better, put yourself into these two scenarios:

1

You're at the circus, having a great time, when all at once the ringmaster announces that you have been selected to fill in for the Tiger Tamer (who's out sick with the flu). You think it's a joke until several strong individuals climb up into the audience, hoist you onto their shoulders, carry you down to the tiger cage, and toss you inside. You look at the tigers, the tigers look at you (lunch!), and inside you a scream starts to build... "get me out of here NOW!!!!!"

2

You're at the circus, minding your own business, when suddenly the announcer says that you're the Tiger Tamer for the day. Luckily you've been to Tiger Tamer School. You have the skills and expertise to do the job. To you, the challenge looks like fun. You get up and excitedly rush down to the tiger cage.

In each case, the tigers are the same. What's different is how you perceive them. That depends on your understanding of the situation and your tiger management (stress management) skills. Without stress management skills, it can feel as if there are invisible tigers everywhere. Those skills make all the difference between experiencing too much stress and enjoying your life.

FEARS, MISCONCEPTIONS, AND WORRIES

Since the way you see the world is a major contributor to your stress level, it's important to identify your fears, misconceptions, and worries. If every fear or worry is a tiger, you can easily become your own worst stressor.

How do you perceive the challenges in your world? What are some of your worries or anxieties—real or imaginary, rational or irrational? Answers to these questions may point you toward things you need to learn or skills you need to develop.

Take a few moments to think about your fears, then list them on a piece of paper. What do they tell you about your life? About yourself?

It would be great if you could understand and handle all of the things that make life difficult, but that isn't always possible. Even people who seem to be competent and confident have times when they feel anxious or overwhelmed. Later in this book, you'll learn ways to take care of yourself during those times and build skills that make the world less intimidating. But for now, let's look at some of the common beliefs that may be increasing the stress in your life.

12 MISCONCEPTIONS THAT GUARANTEE TROUBLE

We all have moments when we're anxious or afraid. Those moments are made worse because of popular misconceptions about stress. See if any of the following statements sound familiar to you. Can you tell why they represent faulty thinking and lead to trouble? Try to figure out the answers before you read them.

1. I can think my way out of feeling bad.
2. I must be crazy for thinking/feeling the way I do.
3. If I keep busy, I'll eventually feel better about myself.
4. If I tell my (mom, dad, school counselor, friend) about how I feel, he/she won't care, understand, or support me.
5. I need to handle these fears and problems by myself. If I ask for help, that proves that I'm not (smart, competent, good enough).
6. It is not okay to cry.
7. If I can get through today, tomorrow is bound to be better.
8. I should be able to figure things out by myself.
9. Life is so serious.
10. All I need is to be left alone for a while.
11. I don't have time to eat right, relax, or play.
12. Other people always know what's best for me.

Misconceptions make problems worse. They slow you down. They give your tigers a chance to gain on you. Here's why:

1. **I can think my way out of feeling bad.** Wrong! Feelings are not something you think yourself into having. You just have them. You need to be aware of them, understand what they are telling you, and, if possible, share them with someone you trust.

2. **I must be crazy for thinking/feeling the way I do.** False! You're not crazy. You're a sane person with a lot of tigers in your life, and you're probably approaching the limit of what you can cope with by yourself.

3. **If I keep busy, I'll eventually feel better about myself.** Untrue! Problems that are ignored don't usually go away or get better on their own. If staying busy is the way you deal with problems, you'll have to be a complete workaholic during the most challenging times of your life.

4. **If I tell my (mom, dad, school counselor, friend) about how I feel, he/she won't care, understand, or support me.** It's possible that some of the important people in your life won't care, understand, or support you...but someone will. Who are the people you really trust? Try talking to them. Being alone with your problems is a prescription for trouble.

5. **I need to handle these fears and problems by myself. If I ask for help, that proves that I'm not (smart, competent, good enough).** See #4 above. It's dumb to handle big problems alone, and smart to reach out for help when you're at your limit. You *can* ask for help; you just have to know who to ask. Who do you feel close to?

6. **It is not okay to cry.** Not only is it definitely okay to cry, but crying can be good for you. It's a tried-and-true way to release pent-up feelings. People often say that they feel better after a good cry. On the other hand, if you're crying too much or too often, you probably need the support of a good friend or counselor.

7. **If I can get through today, tomorrow is bound to be better.** Maybe...and maybe not. Tomorrow might be the same or worse, and you'll have less energy for coping than you do today. The best strategy is to deal with problems and challenges as soon as you become aware of them.

8. I should be able to figure things out by myself. Who says? It's hard to know what to do when you are part of the problem. It's difficult to be objective about yourself. Even counselors get professional help when they have problems. You will probably find it very helpful to talk with someone who can be objective.

9. Life is so serious. True, life has serious times, but if you're not having some fun, being silly, and regularly feeling good about your life and yourself, something is out of balance.

10. All I need is to be left alone for a while. Being alone can be helpful sometimes. But if you're usually by yourself and you rarely talk to anyone, you can get even more out of touch with reality. Friends aren't just "nice to have." We need them for balance, objectivity, and feedback.

11. I don't have time to eat right, relax, or play. Eating right, relaxing occasionally, and having fun on a regular basis are the minimum self-care tools for a resilient, stress-resistant person. A car won't run long on bad fuel at high RPMs, and you can't handle a challenging life on cola and chips.

12. Other people always know what's best for me. The key word here is "always." There are times when it's best to ask others for input or help, and times when you should trust yourself. It's best to have both options. Don't "always" assume you can't think for yourself; don't "always" assume you must go it alone.

WORRY TAPES

Worrying is another way to make things worse for yourself. Like endless-loop cassette tapes, worries play your fears and misconceptions over and over in your mind.

All teenagers are full of concerns about grades, graduating, staying safe, being different, the future, the planet, how they look, and having friends...just for starters. Here's a sampling of what some young people have said they worry about:

- "My parents are fighting again. They've been fighting a lot lately. Maybe this means that they're going to get a divorce...what if they do?"
- "I want to go to the party, but I'm afraid I'll do something stupid and look like an idiot."
- "I'm afraid of being rejected."
- "I'm never going to get all of my homework done."
- "I don't think anyone really understands me."
- "Where am I going to get the money?"
- "I'm afraid I'll get hurt if I care too much for someone."
- "What if nobody ever likes me? I don't want to be alone for the rest of my life."
- "I'm tired of being teased about my grades."
- "I worry about gang fights—I don't want to get beat up or shot or stabbed."
- "I'm sick of fighting stereotypes."
- "The environment will be totally destroyed by the time I'm an adult."
- "I don't want to end up in a dead-end job after high school."

Worries are like little tigers in your head—mini-fears that wear you down emotionally and physically. Having a lot of worries gradually increases the amount of stress you feel. Worrying is not constructive problem-solving! It creates the *illusion* that you're working on your problems, but all it really does is take up your time, tense up your body, drain your energy, and destroy your positive attitude. Worrying doesn't improve your life one bit.

"Worry often gives a small thing a big shadow."
Anonymous

HOW TEENAGERS COPE WITH STRESS

Young people today have complicated lives, challenges, things to worry about, anxieties, fears, pressures to perform and conform, and a headful of misconceptions that make things worse. So how do they survive?

They cope. They use positive coping strategies (and quite a few not-so-positive coping strategies) to get through the hard times. As you'll learn later in this book, coping and stress management are not the same. But coping is what most people do to survive.

When young people were asked how they cope with stress, here's what they said:

- "I read a book or write in my diary." (Mary, 14)
- "I stomp around the house and pound on my brother." (Tim, 15)
- "I ignore it until it blows over." (Sharon, 16)
- "I drink and smoke." (Aaron, 16)
- "I punch a pillow and cry." (Jennifer, 12)
- "I get away from it all with my friends." (Holly, 17)

- "I listen to the white noise of blank tapes until I've calmed myself down." (Lynn, 16)
- "I run until I can't run anymore." (Miguel, 13)
- "I watch my favorite movie for the zillionth time." (Jake, 15)
- "I crank up my music so loud I can't hear my thoughts." (Stormie, 17)
- "I play video games for hours." (Rob, 13)
- "I turn on the computer and surf the Internet." (Zachary, 14)
- "I talk to myself." (Dan, 14)
- "I try to stay organized and on top of things." (Melissa, 16)
- "I watch TV and eat, eat, eat." (Nan, 15)
- "I play the piano, go for a walk, or take a bath." (Tina, 15)
- "I go for a bike ride." (Jonah, 15)
- "I sleep through the evening and get up late at night when the house is quiet." (Willie, 15)

Most teenagers are doing their best to cope with stress, using the skills they have. You can think of coping as a *short-term* way to do something about the *feeling* of being stressed. None of these actions fix the problem that caused the stress in the first place, and some create new problems. But for the moment, at least, they give you a way to decompress or get away from the uncomfortable feeling of stress.

There's nothing wrong with coping activities, as long as they don't go on forever. Unfortunately, it's easy to string them together for hours, days, months, or a lifetime to avoid dealing with the real problems that are driving the stress. It's like using your finger to plug a leak in a dam. It works for a while, and then the growing pressure behind the dam breaks through in another place, and another, and another.... At some point, you run out of fingers.

There are three basic levels of coping strategies: *distraction*, *avoidance*, and *escape*. Some of the activities within each level are good for you, and some are not. It all depends on why you use them and how long you use them.

DISTRACTION

Watching TV, phoning a friend, eating, listening to music, taking a bath, going for a walk, reading a book, even studying can all be distractions. Each of these actions creates a short-term diversion from the anxieties that accompany the challenges in your life.

Distractions are the least drastic and shortest-lived coping activities. They are also relatively harmless.

AVOIDANCE

Avoidance activities are distractions carried to an extreme. They take up more of your time and energy and enable you to sidestep your troubles for longer periods.

Going on a date can be a pleasant activity and a way to avoid worrying about the big test on Monday. However, if you have four dates on one weekend, or if you get so involved with another person that you don't have time for anything else, you are probably avoiding your fear about the test.

Listening to music can be relaxing and a pleasant distraction from the problems of living. On the other hand, going everywhere with your headphones on is a way to avoid human contact and drown out the voices of worry in your own head. When you are using music as a way of shutting out other people and your own self-talk, the stress will continue to build.

Some serious avoidance activities can look good on the outside. A young woman who is the star center on the basketball team may seem to have a great life. What people may not see is how lonely she is. She'd like to have some really close friends, but she doesn't have the time or the know-how to build those relationships. She copes by practicing basketball every spare moment and avoiding her feelings of loneliness.

She is living a *vicious circle*. The more she practices, the lonelier she gets. The lonelier she gets, the more she practices. The more involved in basketball she becomes, the less time she has for making close friends.

The more *you* avoid *your* underlying problems, the worse they get and the more dramatic your avoidance activities become. When you are caught up in this vicious circle, it closes in on you from all sides, growing tighter and tighter. Because you are so busy trying to keep it all together, you may not notice that things are getting worse in a hurry.

In addition to over-involvement in activities, there are four more avoidance strategies that have the potential to become vicious circles: *procrastination, illness, sleep,* and *withdrawal.*

> **"Avoidance is only a vacuum that something else must fill."**
> Shirley Hazzard, *The Bay of Noon*

PROCRASTINATION

Everyone procrastinates. Some of the smartest, most motivated, most successful people in the world today are known (or secret) procrastinators.

If you're at risk for a high-stress lifestyle, procrastination can be especially dangerous for you. It's like slowly shaking a can of cola. It continues to look the same from the outside, but when you pop the tab...POW! Wet, sticky cola all over the place.

Are you a procrastinator? Here's how some young people answered this question:

- "Yes, and I hate it. I put things off and lose track of everything. It really screws me up!" (Jenny, 16)

- "Oh, yeah! I always put off the boring stuff and do the fun stuff first. I sometimes don't finish the boring (but important) stuff." (Lucy, 12)

- "Yes. I put off homework until I am down to almost no credit for turning it in." (Lila, 13)

- "No, I always do my work on time." (Alex, 13)

- "Definitely. I'm up every Sunday night doing homework I should've done earlier in the week." (Ty, 15)

- "Yeah, but I don't care if I get it done or not." (Marty, 15)

- "I wait until I can count the hours before it's due to get started." (Rachel, 17)

- "No, I get my work planned out and finished ahead of time. I hate to have things hanging over me." (John, 16)

- "Yes, I'm always days behind. I don't start until I'm terrorized by a deadline." (Jenny, 15)

- "I don't feel like answering this right now. Let me get back to you...." (Kelly, 13)

> **"Procrastination is the art of keeping up with yesterday."**
> Don Marquis, *archy and mehitabel*

Occasional "putting it off until later" can be simply a bad habit. Regular procrastination, however, invites a major vicious circle. The more you have to do, the more you want to avoid. Your denial about how much you have to do builds with the number of things that need doing. The circle continues and eventually creates a stress-filled mess of missed deadlines, poor excuses, unfinished business, and confused priorities. You live in a total, continuous panic until something finally explodes.

ILLNESS

Parents often are the ones who teach kids how to use illness as a way out of tough situations. You can probably remember back to when you were a little kid and your parents let you stay home from school because you didn't "feel good." If your performance was convincing, you got to rest on the couch and watch TV. Maybe your parents waited on you or gave you extra attention. Even if you really were a tiny bit sick, it was nice to avoid school and be fussed over for a while.

Now that you're older, it's tempting to revert to those times. It's easy to go from feeling pressured and stressed to feeling queasy and sick. We all would like someone to take care of us and fix things for us.

Be careful! Avoiding life by focusing on your aches and pains can become a habit. Even worse, it can become a vicious circle with serious physical consequences.

The more challenges you face, the more you focus on your physical symptoms. The more you worry about them, the more stress you create, and the more likely it is that serious stress-related disorders can result. Ulcers, digestive problems, allergies, headaches, muscle aches, even high blood pressure can be driven or made worse by stress.

In our culture, being ill is an honorable excuse for getting out of almost anything. Nobody expects you to solve your problems when you're flat on your back. Unfortunately, problems won't go away because you have a sore throat. If illness is your avoidance strategy of choice, you can be setting yourself up for a lifetime of major—and expensive—medical consequences.

SLEEP

Hating to get up on Monday mornings and taking an occasional nap are both perfectly normal. The difference between sleep as an ordinary function and sleep as an avoidance activity is all a matter of degree. Even people who do hard physical labor don't need ten hours of sleep, night after night.

If sleep is your place to hide out from your problems, then you'll constantly have to fight gravity just to stay vertical. The more you sleep, the less you'll get done, and the more you'll have to do when you wake up. When this vicious circle gets rolling, almost any horizontal surface—even the floor—will call out to you to lie down "for a few minutes."

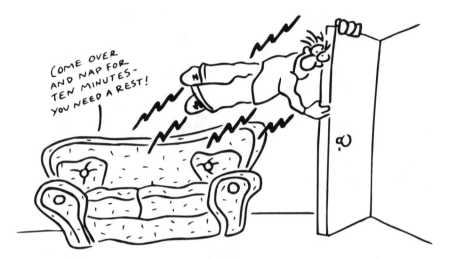

WITHDRAWAL

As your world gets more stressful and you feel tiger breath on the back of your neck, it's natural to want to retreat to a safe place. In fact, withdrawing from the world to regroup, rest, and recover can be good self-care.

It's when you close your door and never come out that withdrawal becomes isolation. Even if you don't have a room of your own, you can shut out other people by not being available to them, by ignoring them, or by refusing to engage with them in any way.

When a little time out becomes a need to *always* be alone—when you try to avoid reality by "going away"—you lose the support and perspective everyone needs when they're having trouble coping. When withdrawal leads to isolation—when you cut yourself off from the balance and objectivity of people who care about you—bad feelings such as anger, fear, sadness, or low self-esteem get worse. A dangerous vicious circle begins and can bring you down in a hurry.

Isolation is the start of the next and most serious coping strategy...*escape.*

ESCAPE

If avoidance is distraction carried to an extreme, escape is avoidance carried to an extreme. Escapist behaviors occur when you reach the limit of your ability to cope with the world around you, the absolute edge of what you can handle. You've done the best you can to deal with the challenges you're facing, using the tools you have, but they aren't enough. Escape behaviors signal that you have lost your way. They indicate that you're a wonderful person (even if you don't feel like one at the moment) who has big problems, and you need help to dig your way out.

Here is how other young people describe what it's like to reach their limits:

- "I want to leave and get away from everything and everyone." (Lynn, 16)
- "I feel like my head is being squeezed into a 1" x 1" cube." (Karen, 16)
- "It's like being on the brink of laughing or crying hysterically." (Kelly, 15)
- "I feel totally destroyed." (Joel, 12)
- "It feels like no one could understand what I'm going through." (Layton, 14)

Severe escapist behaviors can include:

- skipping school or dropping out
- running away from home
- abusing alcohol or other drugs
- developing a compulsive relationship with food, sex, gambling, sports, computers, studying, etc.

- hurting other people
- hurting yourself or attempting suicide.

Escapist behaviors make a mess of your life. They also generate mountains of additional problems that can burden you for years. If you're leaning toward any of the behaviors listed above, *get help.* Find someone you can talk to about what's going on. *Asking for help when you're up against more than you can handle is not a sign of weakness. It's a sign of strength.*

Dealing with the feelings of being stressed, burned out, or at your limit are experiences you'll encounter often during your life. The challenge is not to avoid things that cause stress, but to learn how to handle them in positive, self-affirming ways. It's important to remember that coping is different from acquiring and practicing the lifeskills of stress management. Coping is a short-term way to deal with uncomfortable feelings. All coping is just getting by.

If you're walking around right now with major tiger bites, you may not have the time or energy to develop stress-managing lifeskills. If escape seems like your only option, you need some serious first aid fast. You need Part II, "Self-Care for Tiger Bites."

. . . .

READ MORE ABOUT IT

If you want to know more about helping people with big problems, read:

Feed Your Head: Some Excellent Stuff on Being Yourself by Earl Hipp (Center City, MN: Hazelden Educational Materials, 1991).

Man's Search for Meaning by Viktor E. Frankl (Cutchogue, NY: Buccaneer Books, 1988).

The Power to Prevent Suicide: A Guide for Teens Helping Teens by Richard E. Nelson, Ph.D., and Judith C. Galas (Minneapolis: Free Spirit Publishing Inc., 1994).

Turning People On: How to Be an Encouraging Person by Lewis Losoncy (New York: Prentice-Hall, 1977).

. . . .

PART II

SELF-CARE FOR

TIGER BITES

WHAT TO DO WHEN YOU CAN'T COPE

It's frightening to reach the limit of what you can cope with. It can feel as if you're crazy...or the whole world is crazy. It can seem as if no one understands what you're going through, and you're alone with it all. Your hopelessness can lead you to believe that almost any behavior is justified. It's not! This type of thinking is another signal that you need help, support, and objectivity from people you trust. You are a strong and capable person, but you don't have to solve your problems on your own.

Your first challenge—whether you've just reached your limit or have already started using escapist behaviors—is to *admit that you're in trouble.* This is never easy. When you've been doing your best to handle things, it's hard to acknowledge that your life is not working out so well or that you're unhappy. To protect our self-esteem, most of us have a tendency to lie to ourselves about how we are doing.

Not admitting that you have problems—to yourself or to others—is called *denial.* Denial is a self-delusion and the biggest barrier standing between you, the help you need, and feeling better about yourself and your life. It is a twisted view of reality that strengthens as you decline.

DENIAL
IS NOT A RIVER
IN EGYPT

If you turned to this chapter first, I urge you to reach out for help. *You're worth it.* There are people who can and will see you through your crisis. I promise that you will find someone. Keep looking and don't give up until you do.

If you are able to admit that you're in trouble, congratulations! *Admitting that you are up against more than you can handle is a sign of a psychologically strong person.* There are several things you can do to take care of yourself. Any or all of the following actions will reduce some of the pressure you feel. They can also decrease the chances that you will create additional problems or hurt yourself or others.

GET ANOTHER PERSPECTIVE

If you have even a hint that you're having trouble coping, the healthiest thing you can do is to open up a little and get another person's perspective.

A good way to find out if your behavior is out of line is to ask someone you trust. You'll have to *really* trust the person, because you may not like what you hear.

> *"Linda, do you think I've gone overboard with (homework, dating, studying, sports, being angry, using alcohol or other drugs, being sad, being alone)? I need your honest answer."*
>
> *"Well, now that you ask...."*

Remember that you have been trying your best to keep it all together. You probably have some denial and may not realize how off-center your life has become. Find someone you trust, explain how you feel, then *really listen* to what the other person says. The feedback may point you in the right direction.

It's always better to admit you need help than to continue using the same old self-destructive behaviors.

> **"If you have made mistakes...there is always another chance for you.... You may have a fresh start any moment you choose, for this thing we call 'failure' is not the falling down, but the staying down."**
>
> Mary Pickford

STOP NEGATIVE COPING BEHAVIORS

If you know (or if someone you trust has told you) that your coping behavior is out of line, you might consider stopping whatever it is you're doing. This, too, can be very difficult. Coping is how we avoid the uncomfortable feelings that come with the challenges in life. When you stop a negative coping behavior, you will be left with the feelings you have been avoiding. You may also be face-to-face with some scary issues.

If you're trying to give up a powerful coping behavior—like being compulsive about gambling, drinking, drugs, sex, food, sports, or television—it won't be easy. That's why people who are dealing with big problems seek out support groups. Support from people who have had similar problems and who understand what you're going through is invaluable. Thinking that you can do it alone is what got you into trouble in the first place.

Even issues that are less life-threatening will require real strength to admit and deal with. Behaviors like hiding your social fears behind constant studying, or spending every day after school cleaning your room because your life is chaotic, may not have consequences that are visible or dramatic. But they do limit the quality of your life and cut you off from your true potential.

Once you reach out to get help, you will have ceased making new problems for yourself. As you gradually put yourself and your life back together, a new person will emerge—someone who has better self-understanding, new skills, and, if you're lucky, new people to trust.

> **"Reality is something you rise above."**
> Liza Minnelli

REACH OUT AND TRUST SOMEONE

The most important resource for being resilient is people in your life you can trust. You may be surprised to learn that these people aren't always parents or even best friends. The people who are closest to us are sometimes the *least* objective. They may be so concerned about our feelings and opinions that they don't want to be totally honest with us.

Finding people you can trust takes time and effort. You might want to try a school counselor, a teacher you feel good about, someone from your spiritual community, a distant relative, or even a peer you don't know well but feel you have something in common with. Choose someone, then take a chance. A person who is able and willing to be there for you will let you know by words or actions. How can you tell if someone is completely trustworthy? You probably can't, at least not right away. But if you're at your limit, it may be worth the risk. Reaching out is better than self-destructing.

Trustworthy people help to create a psychologically safe environment where you can be mixed-up, confused, even weird at times. They accept you no matter what. They give you permission to decompress your feelings by expressing them—by crying, getting angry, or being afraid. They tell you the truth about yourself, not just what they think you want to hear. They help you to have a view of the world that is based on reality.

Later in this book, you'll learn how to make and keep close friends. If you don't have a few trustworthy people in your life, you're in trouble. If you have them and don't use them when you've got tiger bites, you're missing a valuable opportunity to take care of yourself.

PLAN TO DEAL WITH PERSONAL ISSUES

Nobody's perfect. Everyone has kinks in their personality— gaps in understanding or skill deficits that guarantee difficulty with some parts of life. These kinks will someday cause frustration and pain. You can deal with them now or wait until you're older, but you *will* have to deal with them.

If you have admitted that your life is a mess, stopped your negative coping behavior, and taken the risk to reach out and trust someone, you may be ready to look at some of these bigger issues in your life—issues like:

- poor study skills
- the inability to form healthy relationships
- not knowing how to stick up for yourself
- not knowing how to prioritize your commitments
- problems expressing anger
- trouble dealing with losses.

No one is born knowing how to study, make friends, be assertive, etc. We all have to learn these skills. Experience is a great teacher, and you may be able to pick up some pointers from your parents or friends. You may be able to learn some of these skills in school or by reading self-help books. You may find classes or support groups where these skills are taught. The trick is not to wait until you're in trouble to learn the skills you need.

There are other, larger life issues—situations you have less or no control over—that can drive self-destructive coping. These include things like:

- drinking, violence, or sexual abuse at home
- the suicide of a friend or family member
- peer pressure or intimidation
- the death of a friend or family member

- watching a friend suffer
- weapons at school
- coping with a physical or mental disability
- discrimination or harassment because of your race, religion, gender, appearance, etc.

These issues all beg for help and support. Trying to handle them on your own can do serious damage to your self-esteem and positive world view...even your personal health or safety.

These problems have the power to be all-consuming. When combined with the normal hassles of daily living, they can quickly wear you down into a puddle of hopelessness. Don't wait until that happens. Get the help and support you need as soon as you realize the problems exist.

> **"You never find yourself until you face the truth."**
> Pearl Bailey

BE GOOD TO YOURSELF

Reaching your limit is similar to being injured. What you need most at times like these is gentle, nurturing care. You might be able to get it from other people, but most likely you'll have to give it to yourself. Here are some ways to be good to yourself when you're in a tough place:

1. **Lower your expectations of yourself.** When your coping resources are wearing thin, you can't possibly be at your best in anything, much less everything. It's okay to lower your expectations of how well you have to do to be an acceptable human being. Some people might say that if you get up in the morning and breathe, you're doing an adequate job. Try

to stay focused on the things that have to be done, and be generous when evaluating your performance. Be at least as good to yourself as you would be to any other person who is feeling down and having a hard time.

2. **Make time for people you like.** Who makes you laugh? Who knows how to have fun? It's energizing to be with people who make you feel good about yourself and life. Stay away from people who are negative, hopeless, and into self-destructive behavior. They can infect you with a gloomy attitude and take you farther away from the help you need to deal with your problems.

3. **Eat right, exercise, and take time to relax.** These actions are gifts you give yourself in the best of times. In the worst of times, when you're totally stressed-out, they become survival skills. In Part III, "Lifeskills," you'll find specific suggestions to try.

4. **Use positive self-talk.** Speaking of negative people, how's your own self-talk? Is it full of angry, demeaning, hurtful statements? If so, you may need to create a list of positive statements to tell yourself. Some examples:

- "I am a good person."
- "I deserve to be treated with respect."
- "I am talented and creative."
- "I am excited about the life I am creating."
- "With help from others, I can handle my problems."

Whenever you hear yourself using negative self-talk, substitute the self-affirming statements. The way to start healing is by loving and believing in yourself. Positive voices in your head can be very helpful in building your self-esteem and reducing your stress.

BELIEVE IN LIFE'S GOODNESS

Do you believe that the world is basically good or basically bad? Neither belief is 100 percent accurate, but believing that things are totally negative sets you up for a tough time. What you see is what you get. If you're always looking for what's wrong with school, your family, your friends, or yourself, you create a bleak world for yourself and increase your stress.

When you're feeling overwhelmed and out of control, it's easy to slip into hopelessness. It's tempting to climb into your self-pity bag and start complaining about your miserable life. Soon you're feeling down about yourself, your life, and the world.

The opposite works, too. When you believe that the world is basically a good place, where good things happen and people are generally thoughtful and kind, life looks better. When you can see what's wonderful about your life, the people around you, and especially yourself, you're in a much stronger position to deal with hard times.

Choosing to see the positive side of life—and it *is* a choice—is your responsibility. In his book, *Man's Search for Meaning,* Viktor Frankl describes his experiences in a concentration camp. He points out that even in the worst conditions imaginable, one can still make choices about one's attitude and view of life. He notes that in the camp, "the prisoner who had lost faith in the future—his future—was doomed. With his loss of belief in the future, he also lost his spiritual hold; he let himself decline and become subject to mental and physical decay." Frankl learned that a person can have everything taken from him or her but one thing: "the last of the human freedoms—to choose one's attitude in any given set of circumstances, to choose one's own way."

You can start strengthening your positive attitude by creating a list of things in your life for which you feel grateful. A list of Gratitude Factors might include:

■ having a safe, comfortable place to sleep at night

■ eating regularly

- being healthy
- having access to clean clothes
- living in a democracy.

Already you're better off than many people. Now add these to your list:

- being able to read
- being able to buy groceries instead of hunting for your food
- having friends who care about you
- having adults who care about you
- having access to a school and the opportunity to learn
- having a TV or radio to help you stay in touch with what's going on in the world.

By now you're *way* ahead of many people in the world.

Take this list one step further: Add to it the specific things that are good about *your* life. Then read the list over again. Suddenly it's a strong statement against feeling sorry for yourself.

If you create your list when you're in a great mood, you can use it as a life preserver during the down times.

WHEN TO USE SELF-CARE

It's crazy to wait until *after* people have major problems to give them the help they need, but that's often what happens in our culture today. You can do better. You can use self-care when you sense that you're *approaching* your limit—as soon as your life starts to be or feel out of control.

As you understand more about yourself and how you cope with stress, you'll become more aware of when you're approaching unacceptable stress levels. You'll also get better at doing something about it.

The real art of being a resilient person goes beyond self-care alone. It comes from learning specific skills that can reduce the stress in your life, along with other skills that set you on a course of self-discovery. These skills make a big difference in the joy and satisfaction you experience as you create the life you want. You'll learn about them in Part III, "Lifeskills."

....

READ MORE ABOUT IT

If you want to know more about the topics covered in this section, write or call:

Rosen Publishing Group
29 East 21st Street
New York, NY 10010
1-800-237-9932

Rosen offers books for young people on a variety of topics including study skills, substance abuse, peer pressure, death, disabilities, and positive thinking. Request a copy of their catalog.

If you could use some tips and suggestions on how to develop good study skills, read:

School Power: Strategies for Succeeding in School by Jeanne Shay Schumm, Ph.D., and Marguerite Radencich, Ph.D. (Minneapolis: Free Spirit Publishing, 1992).

If you're dealing with the death of a friend, read:

When a Friend Dies: A Book for Teens about Grieving & Healing by Marilyn E. Gootman, Ed.D. (Minneapolis: Free Spirit Publishing, 1994).

....

PART III

LIFESKILLS

TAMING YOUR TIGERS

In Part I, "Life in the Jungle," you learned that coping is the way most people survive in a world full of tigers. Coping lets you avoid the stressful feelings associated with the problems and challenges in your life. It's about feeling better in the short run.

Stress management, on the other hand, is about *having a life with less stress over the long term.* "Management" means knowing how to handle some of life's predictable stress-creating situations. If you're tired of feeling tiger breath on the back of your neck, stress management is the best way to get relief, tame some of your tigers, and turn the jungle into more of a playground.

Part III, "Lifeskills," can help you become a stress management wizard. Here you'll discover tried-and-true skills that can give you a better attitude, more self-esteem, and more control over the quality and direction of your life. Obviously, this won't happen just because you read the words on these pages. What you will get from this book is a map of the territory, some sense of what you need to learn, and a push in the right direction. Some of the skills are easy to learn, and you can start using them right

PRRRRRRRR

away. Others will take more time to develop and a lifetime of practice to refine and perfect.

You can cope with stress-related feelings endlessly, but learning and developing stress management skills is the *only* way to reduce the overall level of stress in your life.

Here's what you'll need to get started:

- **A structured approach to learning.** As you learn about stress management skills, talk to your family or teachers about your interest. Ask how they might help you to learn more. Ask a librarian to help you find books, magazine and journal articles, videos, and audios. You might even consider taking a community education class on stress management. To develop any new skill, you need to study it and really understand it.

- **A supportive environment.** Learning new skills takes practice. You'll need help, support, and feedback from others as you experiment and make mistakes. Talk with your parents and teachers. Ask for their support. Practice makes the difference between learning about a skill and having the skill.

■ **Patience.** It takes time to develop new skills. While some of the ideas you'll discover here will yield immediate benefits, others will take longer. Practice, be patient, and eventually you'll notice a difference. Meanwhile, be gentle with yourself. Give yourself permission to do things less than perfectly at first. When Thomas Edison was asked what it was like to have failed a thousand times at trying to invent the light bulb, he replied, "I have never failed. I have learned a thousand ways how *not* to invent a light bulb!"

Don't worry if you don't have a learning plan, a practice schedule, or even patience at this point. Just keep reading. If something looks interesting to you, you'll find a way to learn it.

> **"No limits but the sky."**
> Miguel de Cervantes, *Don Quixote*

TAKING CARE OF # 1

Since stress is something that happens inside of you, it's logical to begin your stress management program by taking better care of your body and mind. Exercise, diet, and relaxation are all important to your well-being.

These lifeskills are fairly easy to learn about, but making them part of your life can be a challenge. Even in your early attempts, however, you'll get a quick return on your time-and-energy investment. These skills are a great way to start managing stress because you can do them on your own and you can start right now.

USE IT OR LOSE IT

With all the emphasis today on professional, competitive sports and athletics, having a *reasonable* activity program hardly seems worth it. But regular physical activity is one of *the* most important stress-fighting skills you can develop. It's especially helpful during times of high stress, when your body is filled with fight-or-flight chemicals. Being active ("taking flight") uses the chemicals your body has produced. Letting them "sit there" can leave you feeling anxious and restless.

Do you have a fitness activity? Why or why not? Here's how some young people answered these questions:

- "Yes. If I don't have anything physical going on, I lose my energy in a hurry." (Karna, 14)

- "No. I'm active enough in my everyday life." (Jon, 18)

- "If I don't stay active, I get tired, out of shape, and my brain turns to mush." (Alissa, 15)

- "What else am I supposed to do after school?" (Eric, 17)

- "Yes, so I can stay in shape. I also take out my frustrations on a set of weights or the tackling dummy." (Joel, 16)

- "I bike a lot. School sport activities don't interest me because I don't like the competition." (Devorah, 14)

- "No. I dislike getting dirty and sweaty." (Judy, 17)

- "I do a lot of physical activity. It's the one thing that keeps me healthy and my mind clear." (Elizabeth, 16)

- "Having a physical release is an absolute must in maintaining a sane life." (Jennifer, 17)

- "I feel good about being active. It's fun, it lets out aggression, and it gives me time to think about things." (Karen, 18)

To get the maximum fitness and stress management benefits from physical activity, you have to be active *on a regular basis.* Notice that I'm not using the words "exercise," "effort," "feel the burn," or "no pain, no gain."

> **"I meet many people who get all fired up to begin an exercise program, only to give up after a few weeks. Inevitably, the reason turns out to be that they selected an exercise not suited for them or that they over-exercised, or both."**
>
> Covert Bailey, *Fit or Fat*

Developing a reasonable activity program involves two basic steps:

1. Find one or more physical activities that you enjoy.
2. Do them regularly at an intensity level that is comfortable, non-abusive, and worthy of a long-term commitment.

In other words, figure out what you like, then enjoy your activity (or activities) on a regular basis. Before you know it, you'll be feeling more fit, relaxed, and better about yourself.

Almost any kind of steady physical activity will do. If you like to walk, walk. If you love to swim, swim. If you'd rather run, run. *Anything* is better than napping on the couch and dreaming about becoming physically active. (Trying to get up off the couch does *not* count as sit-ups!)

To design your personal fitness program, follow the FIT formula:

■ "F" stands for *Frequency*—the number of times per week you should be doing your activity.

■ "I" stands for the *Intensity* level appropriate for you.

■ "T" stands for *Time*—how long each session should last.

FREQUENCY

The minimum amount of activity required to maintain fitness and keep your stress chemistry under control is three sessions a week. Being active three times a week trains your body to do more than just exist. Anything less means that you are actually losing fitness, or at best staying even. More or longer activity sessions will be required if you want to improve your fitness level.

By three sessions, I don't mean three hours on Monday and nothing for the next six days. Instead, spread your activity over the week. Sometimes, after an especially hard day, a little physical activity will help you to slow down, relax, and even sleep better. Whatever form of movement you choose, regular activity lets your body know that you're serious about getting in shape. The time off between sessions allows for rest and physical recuperation.

INTENSITY

In our culture, everyone seems in a hurry to get somewhere, achieve something, and compete with other people along the way. Be careful not to bring that type of thinking to your activity program. As you begin, you may be tempted to go faster or farther or be better than someone else. You may even find yourself competing with yourself by constantly working to beat your previous times or distances.

Pushing yourself is the quickest way to burn out and lose all the benefits of being active. Leave your hard-driving, high-achieving, competitive self at home.

To keep your good intentions from going down the drain, start by determining the most appropriate intensity level for you. You can measure this in two ways: by calculating your target heart rate, or by whistling while you work out.

Your target heart rate (THR) is the specific pulse rate that offers you the maximum benefit during periods of activity. Contrary to popular belief, working harder isn't necessarily better. Your THR is the perfect intensity level for you. You can figure it out with this formula:

$$\frac{(220 - \text{your age}) \times 70\%}{6} = \text{Your THR}$$

The top part of the formula determines your target heart rate per minute. You divide it by 6 because in checking your pulse, you only count for 10 seconds. After that, a healthy heart is already beginning to return to its normal rate.

To determine how close you come to your magic number, spend about 20 minutes at your chosen physical activity. Then check your pulse rate at your wrist or at the carotid artery alongside your Adam's apple.

■ If you're *above* your target heart rate or out of breath, you're pushing yourself too hard. Slow down and try to enjoy yourself more.

- If you're *below* your target heart rate, you're taking it too easy. Turn up the pace and check again.

- If you are *at or close to* your target heart rate, you've found the intensity level you want to maintain during your activity sessions.

Another way to approach the perfect intensity level for you is by whistling while you work out. Basically, if you can whistle (or sing, or carry on a conversation) during your activity session, you'll get all the fitness benefits without risking overdoing it.

Is overdoing it a problem? Probably not in terms of physical danger because you're young and resilient. However, overdoing it is hard work, not fun, and it doesn't feel good. Most often, it leads you back to the couch in front of the TV.

TIME

To get the most out of your physical activity, you need to keep your heart going at or near your target rate for a minimum of 20–30 minutes nonstop. A "work-hard-then-take-it-easy, work-hard-then-take-it-easy" activity doesn't fit the nonstop rule. That's why swimming, walking, jogging, and jumping rope are better fitness sports than tennis and softball. You need to start moving and keep moving, uninterrupted, for about half an hour. Spend a few minutes before and after warming up and cooling down.

To sum up the FIT formula: Aim for three 20–30 minute sessions a week of continuous physical activity, doing something you enjoy, at an intensity level that is comfortable for you. Not a bad assignment, and considering the benefits, well worth the investment.

SOME BENEFITS TO BEING "FIT"

- As your fitness level improves, your body gets better at burning rather than storing fat—at turning calories into energy.

- Because your body gets better at burning fat, you store less fat on your body. If you're not in a regular physical activity program, you are probably highly skilled at storing fat.

- When you're active, you're more efficient at using the fuel stored in fat and carbohydrates. You're not as hungry, you eat less, and when you do eat, you naturally crave foods that are better for you.

- Your heart, lungs, muscles, and other vital parts get stronger and better at what they do. You'll add somewhere between two to ten years to your life expectancy.

- During sustained activity, your body sweeps out any chemicals it produces during the fight-or-flight response. After a reasonable workout, you feel more mellow and relaxed. Your overall attitude improves.

- Because you're doing something good for your body and spirit, you feel good about yourself. Over time, this contributes to growing self-esteem.

These reasons make physical activity one of the most important stress management skills you can develop. If you have any difficulty starting your program, ask your Health or Physical Education teacher for inspiration and advice. These educators know a lot about fitness and are often good role models. They can also be a great source of objectivity and support as you make long-range plans for getting fit and staying fit.

. . . .

READ MORE ABOUT IT

If you want to know more about fitness, read:

Aerobics Basics by Karen Liptak (Englewood Cliffs, NJ: Prentice-Hall, 1983).

Kid Fitness: A Complete Shape-Up Program from Birth through High School by Kenneth H. Cooper (New York: Bantam Books, 1991).

The New Fit or Fat by Covert Bailey (Boston: Houghton Mifflin Co., 1991).

. . . .

YOU ARE WHAT YOU EAT

As long as you're going to become a relaxed but high-energy and active person, you may as well put good fuel in your tank. What you eat affects how you feel, and some consumables can actually increase your anxiety and stress.

For many teens, the four basic food groups are Fast, Sweet, Carbonated, and Everything Else. It's the last category that includes the stuff that's really good for you. Unfortunately, in our crazy, hurry-up world, it's too easy to grab what's available, and that usually means junk foods.

If you've studied biology in school, you may recall that every cell in your body is affected by what you eat. Skin cells, muscle cells, blood cells, nerve cells, even brain cells know the difference between a carrot and a cola. If you don't treat your cells right, they will eventually get their revenge.

Healthy eating is a skill. You don't have to be a rocket scientist to know what's good for you and what's not, but it does take personal commitment and a willingness to learn some of the facts about food. A special kind of self-respect is required to avoid the garbage and invest the extra effort in finding health-building food.

If you already have a little of that kind of motivation, there are two things you can do, starting now, to make a huge difference in how stressed you feel: *Reduce your caffeine use* and *reduce your sugar use.*

HIPPITY-HOP

Caffeine in its pure state is a white, bitter-tasting, crystalline substance that belongs to the group of naturally occurring stimulants called *methylxanthines*. Methylxanthines are found in coffee beans, tea leaves, kola nuts, and cocoa beans.

Caffeine is a mysterious drug that pops up everywhere. It's "hidden" in places like chocolate, cold capsules, cough syrups, and cocoa. The biggest pusher of this drug for kids is canned soda (pop). Readily available in schools, malls, and quick shops, it's often loaded with caffeine. Unless the can says "caffeine free," it probably isn't.

When young people were asked, "Do you use caffeine?," here is what some of them said:

- "Pot after pot after pot." (Daniel, 17)
- "No. I don't like being high on chemicals of any kind." (Billy, 17)
- "Not much—a couple of colas, maybe four or five cups of coffee in a day." (Tanya, 16)
- "I don't feel well when I use it. I get too jumpy." (Ginger, 16)
- "As much as I can get my hands on." (Taylor, 14)
- "I take four caffeine pills every morning to get through the day." (Rochelle, 15)
- "No. Caffeine stains your teeth." (Amy, 15)
- "Yes, if I have things to do and I'm dead tired." (Michelle, 17)
- "No. I don't like the taste and I'd rather not get addicted." (Elizabeth, 16)

Most young people report at least some use of caffeine, and many report a lot.

Caffeine creates an artificial, temporary lift for people who are stressed-out, a kind of "energy" very different from the type you get with a physically active lifestyle. Like any mood-enhancing drug, the quick "up" gives you the illusion that you feel better than you actually do. A stressed person who is a little depressed can pretend to feel normal with a continuous low blood level of caffeine. Four to five cans of cola or cups of coffee a day will almost do it, but that's a risky way to take care of business.

Why is caffeine a problem drug? Because it leads to a physical reaction very similar to the fight-or-flight response. Too much of it makes you edgy and jittery. It turns up the volume on your worry tapes so things seem worse than they really are. If you overdo caffeine by even a little, you may soon be looking over your shoulder for invisible tigers.

Some of the signs of excess caffeine intake may include restlessness, nervousness, irritability, the shakes, sleeplessness (and/or scary dreams), sweaty hands and feet, irregular heartbeat, having to go to the bathroom all the time, nervous or upset stomach, intestinal disturbances, and, at high levels, an irresistible urge to hippity-hop all over the place.

If these sound like the symptoms of excess stress, that's because they're very similar. When you're loaded up on caffeine, it's hard to tell whether your anxieties are due to your upcoming math test, the fight you just had with your friend, or the four cups of coffee you gulped an hour ago. *Using caffeine is like drinking nervousness in small doses.*

The students we surveyed also reported another caffeine-related cost: headaches. Headaches driven by blood pressure or tight muscles in the head and face are often associated with too much stress. But headaches can also come from too little caffeine if your body is used to regular doses. Like many other drugs, caffeine is addictive. You need to use more and more to get the same effect, and when you cut back or quit using, you experience withdrawal symptoms.

Depending on your body size and chemistry, it's possible to get hooked on caffeine at a consumption level between 200–400 milligrams per day. That's equivalent to four cans of regular cola (or any other soft drink that contains caffeine) or four cups of coffee.

How can you tell if you're a caffeine junkie? Try going without it for a few days. If you get a headache and coffee or cola relieves it, you're addicted. The good news is: If you don't go for a caffeine fix, the withdrawal headaches will go away by themselves...after a few really miserable days.

You may be amazed to learn that some of America's favorite headache pain relievers are loaded with caffeine. They give temporary relief while quietly increasing the intensity of your addiction. Strange but true...and legal.

RIDING THE SUGARCOASTER

Caffeine is a bad partner if you're dealing with tigers in your life. But it has a close friend, and they are often found together.

Sugar by any other name—glucose, sucrose, fructose, or corn syrup—tastes as sweet. No matter what form it takes, it can generate subtle (and not-so-subtle) mood swings. It can leave you feeling giggly one moment and sleepy the next.

Because processed sugars are so chemically potent, your body absorbs them into the bloodstream very quickly. This gives you a wonderful buzz that can brighten a gloomy, boring moment and light up your life...for about an hour.

What's behind the "sugar high?" The sudden boost in blood sugar surprises your pancreas. Your average pancreas is a calm and stable organ. Its job is to maintain a normal level of sugar in the blood stream. So you can imagine the excitement when all of a sudden—*bam!*—incoming sugar in mega-doses sets off the alarm. While you're getting the rush of sugar-driven energy, your pancreas jumps into high gear, secreting insulin to trap the excess sugars and carry them off to the liver.

Because of all the excitement, and because your pancreas wants to do a good job, it sometimes puts out too much insulin and removes too much blood sugar. That sends you back into the head-nodding doldrums. You get sleepy and cranky, and soon the vending machine is calling to you from down the hall.

You have just strapped yourself into the front seat of the Sugarcoaster. Up (sugar rush), down (sugar crash), up (sugar rush), down (sugar crash)—and on and on it goes. The problem is that each down takes you deeper than the last. By the end of a day on the Sugarcoaster, you're wiped out. And that's when a caffeine fix begins to seem like a good idea.

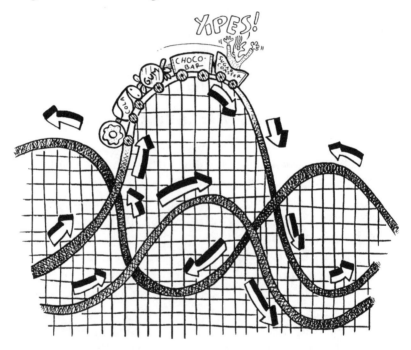

When you combine a lot of sugar and a hit of caffeine, you have a prescription for physical and emotional confusion. You already know about caffeine, but did you know that a can of cola contains the equivalent of about half of a sandwich bag full of white sugar in highly condensed form? This means a *big* up and *big* down, plus all the problems of caffeine.

One chemical (sugar) picks you up and later drops you off a cliff into a mild depressive state. Meanwhile, the other (caffeine) strings you out with artificial energy that gives you headaches and exaggerates your problems.

How much sugar does the average American consume each year? *128 pounds.*

"Sugar is like puppy love that makes your teeth rot."
Scott Knickelbine, *The Low-Cost No-Fuss All-Natural Food Guide for Students (and Other Desperate People)*

In our culture, we get messages that it's okay to use chemicals to feel better. You see them all the time on TV. Plus it's hard not to use caffeine and sugar when they're so readily available and are made to appear so innocent. But the physical and emotional costs of using these chemicals are enormous. Dropping them out of your diet is a challenge, but it's not impossible—and it's worth it.

If you can't stop using either or both of these substances, at least consider reducing your intake. You'll become more physically and emotionally stable and better equipped to do battle with your tigers. Here are a few suggestions to get you started:

■ If you simply must stay up late to study, try brief periods of physical activity to get your blood flowing to your brain. Run in place or do jumping-jacks. If you like the taste of coffee or cola, drink decaffeinated.

■ If your sweet-tooth starts throbbing, munch on fruit. An apple is not a ticket to the Sugarcoaster because the sugars it contains are complex and natural. Your body breaks them down slowly to give you a gradual lift over time.

It isn't easy to let go of old habits and find new ways to energize yourself. But in time you'll feel better physically, and you'll like the person you're becoming.

RABBIT FOOD AND SELF-ESTEEM

Can lettuce make you a better person? Can carrots give you courage? You may find it hard to believe, but the answer to both questions is *yes*—because of what they do for your self-esteem!

It's all tied in with habits. Every one of us is at the mercy of the collection of habits called "my life." This collection of behaviors that we repeat every day has a momentum that keeps going even when we consciously want to do something different. It's like a giant cruise ship. Once it starts moving and picks up speed, it takes a long time to slow down or change course. The captain understands this challenge and doesn't try to make quick stops or turn the ship on a dime.

But we often forget the power of the habits in our lives. When we try to make changes in our "course" too quickly, the momentum of our habits keeps going and knocks our good intentions flat.

If you have ever tried to lose weight, start an activity program, finish your homework earlier, stop smoking, or quit biting your fingernails, you know how hard it can be. Not accomplishing the changes we set out to make can wreak havoc on our self-esteem.

So—back to rabbit food. If once in awhile you eat lettuce and carrots and other stuff that's good for you, this makes you into a person who, little by little, is improving yourself. If you eat right and are physically active on a regular basis, you can say to yourself (or anyone else who'll listen), "I do positive things for myself, and I'm becoming an even more wonderful, healthier person." It's great for the self-esteem and almost *too* simple.

"...it is a peaceful thing to be one succeeding."
Gertrude Stein

The trick to overcoming the force of habit is to make very, very small changes and stick with them. Eating a salad or skipping dessert one day a week will allow you to identify yourself as someone who's growing in a positive way. That is why snacking on carrots instead of candy for one day a week can improve your self-esteem. It can also make you a mysterious and fascinating person in the eyes of your friends.

Once you start working off your nervous energy with physical activity and stop consuming jet fuel, the world will appear to slow down and feel a little less intimidating. Your problems won't seem as large, and some might disappear all together.

But the world will still be a challenging place. The lifeskills that make you healthier aren't all you'll need to be a resilient, stress-resistant person. For those times when you are facing the big challenges of your life, you'll want a reservoir of calm. That comes from having relaxation skills.

. . . .

READ MORE ABOUT IT

If you want to know more about healthy eating, read:

Jane Brody's Good Food Book by Jane Brody (New York: Bantam, 1987).

. . . .

FINDING THE EYE OF THE HURRICANE

We all have moments when life seems overwhelming and we feel uncertain and insecure. It's as if we're alone and caught in a hurricane somewhere out on the ocean. We get rocked by waves of emotion, tossed around by all the things we have to do, and almost blown over by the moods and opinions of others. It's easy to wonder if we can handle it, if our fragile constitutions will weather the storm.

For times like these, there's another important set of lifeskills. These skills can help us find the eye of the hurricane—the place in the middle of the commotion and confusion where things are calm, the sun is shining, and it's a great day.

Relaxation skills can take you there. They can help you to achieve a quiet, deeply restful calm that is soothing to your tattered mind and nourishing for your body. If you practice these skills regularly, you'll learn how to get to that quiet place quickly when you sense a storm of stress approaching.

In addition to being a necessary survival skill, knowing how to relax is essential to maximizing your potential and maintaining your brain in tip-top condition. Never relaxing is like keeping the muscles in your arms constantly tensed. Eventually you lose flexibility and feel so tired that you have trouble doing simple, everyday things like writing, brushing your teeth, and waving good-bye.

Without periods of relaxation, you get "brain lock." You lose your ability to think straight and concentrate, much less generate creative ideas.

> "Rest is not a matter of doing absolutely nothing. Rest is repair."
>
> Daniel W. Josselyn

Just as there are many different physical activities to choose from, there are several types of relaxation skills. They all have three characteristics in common:

1. Because they are skills, they must be learned and practiced. That means you won't be good at them at first, and you'll need to be patient with yourself.

2. They create very noticeable and positive physical and mental changes.

3. They invite you to focus your attention on something besides the constant flow of thoughts your mind produces.

Basically, relaxation is *non-doing*—something a lot of people find difficult. A goal of nearly every relaxation technique is to be physically still while maintaining an alert but neutral mental focus. Other words that may help you to understand this condition include:

■ controlled calm

■ passive attention

■ positive detachment

■ focused rest.

Some of the actions you might think of as "relaxing" may feel good but are basically coping behaviors—pleasant ways to avoid your stressors. Real relaxation provides deep, controlled rest and strengthens your ability to achieve positive mental detachment.

On the following page is a list of some things young people have said they do to relax. See if you can sort out the real relaxation techniques from the coping behaviors and other activities that are no help at all. Identify each option with these letters:

■ "C" for coping

■ "R" for relaxation

■ "N" for no help.

The answers are printed upside down at the bottom of the page.

1. Watch TV
2. Go for a walk
3. Listen to a blank tape
4. Take a nap
5. Eat something
6. Play the piano
7. Concentrate on breathing
8. Read a book
9. Lie in bed and daydream
10. Have a cup of coffee
11. Listen to soft, slow music
12. Do homework
13. Relax muscles one group at a time
14. Call a friend on the phone
15. Meditate
16. Bake cookies

12.C 13.C 14.C 15.R 16.C
1.C 2.C 3.R 4.C 5.C 6.C 7.R 8.C 9.C 10.N 11.C

Did you discover that some things you thought were relaxation techniques were actually coping strategies—or no help at all?

■ Watching TV is *not* a relaxation technique because your brain is busy, your mental focus isn't neutral, and the TV is in charge.

■ Sleep is *not* a relaxation technique because it isn't a controlled state and you're not alert. Also, dreams (especially bad dreams) can cause physical and emotional stress.

■ Reading a book is *not* a relaxation technique because your brain is engaged and your focus is on the printed page.

■ Having a cup of coffee is *not* a relaxation technique.

Watching TV, taking naps, or reading may be pleasant distractions, but they are not real relaxation. Real relaxation is where you are calm, alert, and choosing to maintain a neutral mental focus. Coping strategies make you feel better temporarily because they mask or distract you from anxiety and tension. Real relaxation takes you directly to the eye of the storm, creating deep physical rest and mental calm. The more you practice relaxation skills, the more capable you become of staying centered in quietness during times of stress.

The only real relaxation techniques on the list are *listen to a blank tape, concentrate on breathing,* and *meditate.* All of these are forms of steady non-doing with a neutral mental focus.

While there is no trick to learning relaxation skills, they take a lot of practice. Non-doing doesn't come easily for most of us. But your ability to be a calm and resilient person will be directly proportional to the amount of time you devote to practicing very simple non-activities. Here are two you can try right now.

DEEP BREATHING

Your body and your mind function together. Your thoughts and feelings affect your physical condition. Your physical state influences your attitude and mood.

73

When you're nervous, excited, or angry, your breathing is more rapid and tends to move up in your chest (short, shallow breaths). When you're calm and relaxed, you breathing slows (deep, regular breaths). *Slow, deep, regular breathing is the physical expression of a peaceful mind.*

It's possible to *consciously* manipulate your breathing to achieve a restful mental state—even during times of stress. The script that follows will show you how. You may want to have someone you trust read it to you until you're ready to try it alone. Another option is to record the script in your own voice. That way, the tape will also serve as a timer for the experience.

To prepare:

- Find something comfortable to lie on or sit on.
- Loosen restrictive belts or tight clothing.
- Lie on your back or sit comfortably so your hips and legs relax.
- Close your eyes and get ready to focus on the instructions you will hear.

DEEP BREATHING SCRIPT

Keeping your mouth closed, inhale and exhale deeply through your nose three times.

Now place your right hand on your stomach, just above your belly-button, and your left hand at the top of your chest.

Don't try to manipulate your breathing yet. Just notice where in your body it is coming from.

Now take a long, slow, deep breath into your chest. Your left hand should rise, but your right hand should stay still.

Pause briefly, keeping your chest full, then exhale slowly through your nose.

Notice which muscles are involved, the sensation of fullness at the pause, and the feeling of relaxation that comes with the slow, deliberate release of air.

Repeat this "chest breathing" three times.

Breathe in...hold...release.

In...hold...release.

In...hold...release.

Now take a break. Stop controlling your breathing and let it find its own rhythm and location.

Now take a long, slow, deep breath, this time into your stomach. Your right hand should rise while your left hand stays still. This may feel awkward at first, but be patient.

Repeat this "belly breathing" three times.

Breathe in...hold...release.

In...hold...release.

In...hold...release.

Take another break and let your breathing return to its natural state.

Now, keeping your hands in place, combine all of the breathing movements into one slow, continuous, four-count exercise, like this:

- ▦ *Count "one" and breathe into your belly so your right hand rises. Pause for a mini-second.*
- ▦ *Count "two" and breathe into your chest so your left hand rises. Pause for a mini-second.*

- *Count "three" and begin a controlled, gradual exhalation from your belly so your right hand lowers. Pause for a mini-second.*
- *Count "four" and slowly release the remaining air in your chest so your left hand lowers.*

When you feel you have completely exhaled, pause for a mini-second before you start the cycle again.

Repeat this slow, rhythmic breathing for two to three minutes. Remember to alternate between chest breathing and belly breathing.

When you are done, take a minute to let your breathing return to normal before you get up.

Go through the whole script three or four times until you feel comfortable with it. From then on, you can use the four-count cycle as a stress-reducing breathing exercise.

Focusing on your breathing will probably feel strange at first. Eventually, though, you'll begin to look forward to the calm state you can generate by this simple exercise. As you get used to it (which will take time), you may want to lengthen your sessions. Setting a timer for five or ten minutes will eliminate one more thing to think about.

With practice, this activity will feel natural and comfortable. You'll be able to call on this skill whenever you want to enter the calm eye of the storm.

> **"Nothing can be more useful...than a determination not to be hurried."**
> Henry David Thoreau

MEDITATION

Just as your heart beats endlessly and automatically, day in and day out, your mind produces an endless stream of thoughts. If you don't believe it, try putting a stop to your thinking. Set this book down for a moment, close your eyes, and turn off your brain. Stop thinking...now!

(PAUSE)

Did it work? Probably not. It simply can't be done. Your brain is a highly competent thinking machine. Even when you try to create a quiet space, thoughts keep creeping into your awareness.

Because your thoughts contain all of your fears, worries, and concerns, *you can be one of your own worst stressors.* Although you can't control the flow of your thoughts, you can get some relief from them by skillfully focusing your attention somewhere else.

If you were asked to move your attention to the bottom of your right foot, you'd suddenly become aware of what was going on there. We can shift our attention fairly easily, but learning to shift our mental focus to neutral is *the* primary challenge of all relaxation skills and the heart of most meditation activities. The instructions that follow can help you learn this skill of detaching from your thinking machine.

To prepare:

- Find a firm chair and a blank wall to look at.

- Sit on the chair facing the wall with your back relaxed but straight. This position may feel uncomfortable at first but is much easier over the long run. Your feet should be flat on the floor.

- Fold your hands in your lap or lay them palms-down on top of your thighs.

- Keep your head up and pull your chin in a little to keep your neck straight.

- Keep your eyes open and look down at about a forty-five degree angle. Don't tilt your head; just *look* down.

77

Once you're familiar with this basic posture, you're ready for the instructions. You may want to have someone read them to you while you follow along.

Like deep breathing, meditation takes practice, but it will soon feel friendly and familiar.

MEDITATION INSTRUCTIONS

There are three important rules to remember:

1. *Don't control your breathing. Just let it come naturally.*

2. *Don't move. Your body must remain absolutely still for the entire session. Bodies have a way of becoming distractions if you let them.*

3. *Don't stop before the time is up. Decide before you start how long you want the meditation session to last. In the beginning, 5–8 minutes is enough. Later you may want to lengthen each session to 20 or even 30 minutes. It's helpful to set a timer for this activity so you aren't constantly distracted by looking at a clock. Start with one minute if you like, but don't quit before the time is up.*

When you're comfortable and ready to begin, focus your attention on your breathing. Keeping your mouth closed, silently count "one" on the next inhalation and "two" on the exhalation, "three" on the next inhalation and "four" on the exhalation...and so on up to "ten." When you reach "ten," start over with "one" again on the next inhale.

Don't manipulate your breathing in any way. Just observe and silently count the inhalations and exhalations.

Breathing and counting. You can handle that, right? Actually, this simple action can be much more difficult than you might think. The moment you begin the exercise (assuming you can make a place in your schedule in the first place), you're likely to encounter a whole range of roadblocks. They represent the barriers between your stressed-out self and your potential to be a more serene person.

Roadblock #1: Your Rebellious Mind

What happens: Your mind won't appreciate your attempts to control your focus of attention. It's used to being in charge, driving the bus, going where it wants, and keeping you busy with thinking, worrying, and planning. Just as you settle into the comfort of counting passing breaths, your mind will start sending out invitations—important things for you to consider. Before you know it, your "thinking machine" will be back in charge.

As you get better at staying detached, your mind will find more subtle and clever ways to get your attention. You'll suddenly remember things you have to do. Interesting and creative thoughts will appear. Romantic thoughts, silly thoughts, even old, familiar fears and worries will creep in.

What to do: As soon as you realize that you have been distracted, go back to the focus on your breathing. Begin at "one" and start counting again.

The first few times you try meditating, you'll probably have to go back to "one" a lot. You may never even get to "ten." That's okay. Eventually you'll learn to stay detached from the constant flow of thoughts your thinking machine creates. *The best technique is not to fight your thoughts, but to let them drift past like half-noticed clouds in a summer sky.*

Roadblock #2: Your Rebellious Body

What happens: Your body isn't used to being absolutely still for long periods while you're awake. So, like your mind, your body

79

will do its best to distract you. As you sit there, some body parts will "demand" to be moved, and others will twitch or tingle.

A little physical discomfort will threaten to become unbearable pain. Itches will suddenly develop all over your body. Hunger, thirst, aches...all can become huge problems, if you allow yourself to focus on them. With the body, there is no limit to the potential for distraction.

What to do: Go back to "one" and start counting again. When you realize that you have been distracted by your body, move your attention back to your breathing and focus on counting.

Remember that the body and mind influence each other. All bodily distractions are really the expression of a restless mind. No matter how compelling a physical sensation may seem, it will go away if you cease to feed it with your attention. To date, no one has developed gangrene, paralysis, or any other serious problem because he or she sat still for thirty minutes, much less five!

Roadblock #3: The World

What happens: Somehow the whole world seems to know when you're about to sit down to meditate—and sometimes it seems as if the people in your world have organized to make it difficult for you. Friends stop by or call, people knock on your door, your little brother barges into the room, or the next-door neighbor picks that particular moment to start mowing the lawn or blasting the stereo.

What to do: Go back to "one" and start counting again. When you realize that you have been distracted by the world around you, return your attention to your breathing and focus on counting.

Unless you join a monastery or convent that requires a vow of silence, you'll never find absolute quiet and insulation from the world (and even monasteries and convents have crickets and squeaky hinges). Learning how to detach from distractions is an important benefit that comes from meditation practice.

It may help to choose a time when you can be reasonably sure of not being interrupted. Don't start your quiet time five minutes before dinner. You should also choose a place that's off the beaten track—like a far corner of the house, preferably a room with a door you can shut. You may even want to make a "Do Not Disturb" sign and hang it on the door.

If you think the people around you will understand, you may want to tell them what you're doing. It can be upsetting to see a young person sitting absolutely still, staring at a blank wall, if you don't know what he or she is doing and why.

**"Sometimes I sits and thinks,
and sometimes I just sits."**

Unknown

GOOD REASONS TO PRACTICE RELAXATION SKILLS

Let's assume that you've mastered the art of relaxation. You're so good at it that you can practically turn yourself into jelly by focusing on your breath. You're able to sit calmly and remain serene in the middle of an all-school food fight.

So what? Will the ability to relax eliminate stress from your life or make your wildest dreams come true? Probably not. But relaxation skills will do a lot of other things for you, including but not limited to these:

1. They will help you to feel generally less crazy, worried, and insecure.

2. They will give your body and mind a chance to rest and recover from the stresses and strains of your life.

3. They will help you to re-center yourself in the calm eye of the storm when you're stressed-out and at the limit of what you can handle.

4. They will help you to feel better about yourself, because you're doing something positive to take care of yourself.

Remember that relaxing and detaching are *skills* you learn. Skills take time and practice before you can be good at them. Every practice session will make a small and positive difference while moving you closer to the calm eye of the storm. Be patient with yourself. Enjoy the soothing quiet you are learning to create.

. . . .

READ MORE ABOUT IT

If you want to know more about relaxation, read:

The Relaxation Response by Herbert Benson (New York: Avon, 1976).

The Wellness Book by Herbert Benson (New York: Simon & Schuster, 1993).

. . . .

BEING ASSERTIVE

So far we've talked about things you can do to take better care of #1 (that's you). But there are other lifeskills you can learn that will lower the amount of stress you live with every day. These lifeskills have to do with your relationships with other people.

Do you sometimes feel oppressed by your parents, teachers, peers, or the world in general? Does it seem that your needs, opinions, and feelings don't count? That *you* don't count? If so, you're not alone.

> **"School is an exercise in people abuse."**
> Polly, 18

There are three basic reasons why young people feel oppressed:

■ They don't have a lot of power. Age, physical strength, money, authority, even experience all give other people more power and control in the world. That's just how it is.

■ Life isn't fair. Some school rules, teachers, friends, and family members aren't fair. Intentionally or unintentionally, some people get carried away with their power over others and misuse it. It's not nice, it's not fun, and it can be very frustrating, but that's how it is.

■ Most young people lack the skills they need to defend themselves against intrusive people and unfair situations.

Over the course of your life, you can plan on regular encounters with people and situations in which you will feel threatened and vulnerable. Unless you learn how to protect yourself, to speak up, and to express your feelings in constructive ways, you can expect to be mistreated, taken advantage of, or discounted.

How good are you at sticking up for yourself? Find out by taking this short quiz. Answer each question with "Y" for yes or "N" for no.

1. When a teacher is unfair, do you call it to his/her/someone's attention?

2. When a friend is very (or regularly) late to meet you, do you mention it?

3. When you're in line for lunch or a movie and someone cuts in front of you, do you speak up?

4. Do you confront people who embarrass you?

5. If someone owes you money, do you ask for it?

6. When a friend has a problem, are you able to express your feelings and be supportive?

7. When your teacher makes a mistake in class, are you able to speak up about it in a noncritical way?

8. If your friends all want to do something and you have a different idea, are you able to express it?

9. Can you offer input into family decisions when you don't like what is being decided?

10. Can you discuss the limitations your family imposes on your freedom without being aggressive or having a self-pity tantrum?

If you answered "N" to more than a few of these questions, you may lack important assertiveness skills.

Most people respond to oppressive or demanding situations in one of three ways: by being *passive*, by being *aggressive*, or by being *passive-aggressive*. Each of these response styles has consequences. Before we explore the assertive response style, let's take a look at each of the three common ways of dealing with violations of your rights. See if any of them sound familiar to you.

THE PASSIVE RESPONSE STYLE

Passive people try to avoid trouble. They want everybody to be happy, everything to be nice, and the world to appear conflict-free. They would rather let someone stand on their foot than risk making them angry by asking them to move.

As a result, passive people suffer in silence, don't get their needs met, and eventually become hopeless and depressed. They end up feeling hurt, misunderstood, pressured, and at a deep level, angry. They talk, behave, feel, and sometimes even look like victims. Here are some examples of passive responses:

1

You want good grades, but your teacher only gives out a few high grades every reporting period, "no matter what." Rather than tell her how unreasonable the system feels to you, you work extra hard to get one of the few "A's" available. You feel cheated and anxious every time you go to class.

2

There's a person who threatens you with physical violence on a regular basis after school. Rather than get some help and support to deal with the situation, you put up with it and live in fear every day.

3

A friend borrowed your favorite sweater for a party, and you really want it back. She calls and asks if she can keep it for a little while longer. You say, "Sure, no problem." Weeks go by. Meanwhile, you feel angry every time you see her, but you don't say anything.

Passive people quietly put up with whatever happens to them. They seem to worry more about everyone else's needs than their own. When they do talk about their feelings, it's usually in terms of how bad they have it. They can be highly skilled at suffering. Because they don't know how to defend themselves, passive people are easy prey for oppression, aggression, and abuse.

**"An appeaser is one who feeds a crocodile—
hoping it will eat him last."**
Winston Churchill

Why are some people passive? Here are a few reasons:

- They have not been taught how to be assertive. Being a victim is all they know.
- They fear the loss of approval from others if they make their needs and feelings known.
- They want to avoid conflict and keep peace at all costs.
- They mistake passiveness for being polite or kind.
- They mistake assertiveness for being aggressive or pushy.
- They are uncertain about their basic rights as human beings.

Passiveness has a high price in terms of stress and self-esteem. Passive individuals are almost always stressed-out because they have to be constantly on guard for abusive people and situations. They give up their personal power by focusing too much on other people's needs. They lose their sense of themselves as valuable individuals. They have difficulty in relationships because they can't defend themselves and get their needs met. They become emotional pressure-cookers—insecure, lonely, and resentful.

When young people were asked to define "passive person," here is what some of them said:

- "A vegetable." (Ben, 13)

- "Someone without a personality." (Deborah, 14)

- "Someone who won't stick up for themselves and who depends on others to give their life meaning." (Elizabeth, 16)

- "Someone who is just going through the motions of life." (Karen, 18)

- "A person who can be run over by the whole world." (Dave, 16)

- "Someone who is always saying they're bored." (Jake, 15)

- "A person who can't stand up for themselves even when they're right." (Adam, 14)

- "People without any internal drive. They don't do things; things are done to them." (Miriam, 15)

- "A person who never takes charge, shares ideas, or expresses their feelings." (Nina, 14)

- "Someone to fool with, to have fun at their expense." (LeeRoy, 16)

- "Someone who never disagrees or fights for their beliefs." (Lucy, 12)

- "Silent, still, quiet, sad, dead." (Katie, 13)

THE AGGRESSIVE RESPONSE STYLE

On the other end of the continuum are aggressive individuals. They are loud, pushy, and sarcastic, and they seem to take up more space than other people. They make fun of authority, argue, gossip, tease, and put others down. Because they are so hard to be around, other people don't like them. Here are some examples of aggressive responses:

1

You get a poor grade on a paper because it was supposed to be ten pages long and you only wrote five pages. Instead of explaining that you had trouble finding information on your topic, you tear up the paper, throw it at the teacher, and stomp out of the room.

2

Someone cuts in front of you in the lunch line. You push her out of the way.

3

You don't return a borrowed sweater because you totally trashed it at a party. When the person asks for it back, you laugh and say, "Tough luck, it's been destroyed."

4

Because you broke a family rule, your mom gives you a 9:00 P.M. curfew for a night when your friends are having a party. You go anyway and don't come home until after midnight.

Why are some people aggressive? Here are some possible reasons:

- They have not been taught how to be assertive. They mistake aggressiveness for assertiveness. They confuse power over others with personal power and personal strength.

- They have seen some people get what they want by being mean, taking advantage of others, and disregarding other people's feelings.

- They want to maintain control at all costs. If they don't dominate other people and situations, they think they are being weak and making themselves vulnerable.

- They are unsure about or have never learned about peoples' basic rights. They think they can do whatever they want whenever they want.

Like passiveness, aggressiveness has a price. Because aggressive people get abusive when they hear something they don't like, it's hard to be open with them, so they don't get honest feedback in their relationships. They use power and force to get what they want, and they won't negotiate, so they don't make friends easily. They ignore the needs of others, so they can't keep the friends they make.

Openness, honesty, and respect for others' needs are vital to healthy relationships. As a result, aggressive people tend not to have close, intimate relationships. They feel lonely and detached, angry, resentful, and misunderstood—which makes them more aggressive. They experience a lot of stress because they try to control things and their aggressiveness causes major problems. They have some sense of being in charge of their small universe, but their deeper needs for love and connection with others go unmet.

When young people were asked how they felt about aggressive people, here is what some of them said:

- "Sorry for them." (Ben, 13)
- "I feel like getting aggressive right back. I don't like to be intimidated." (Joel, 16)
- "I get really mad and tell them off or just leave them." (Elise, 15)
- "When someone is aggressive, it causes me to step back from them. I don't feel comfortable around these people." (Elizabeth, 16)
- "I feel hurt." (Rose, 15)
- "Frustrated. I have trouble understanding aggression and violence." (Karen, 15)
- "I get defensive or brush them off, depending on the mood I'm in." (Alicia, 18)
- "I feel angry that anyone would act that way toward anyone else." (Van, 14)
- "I try to ignore them." (Damian, 13)
- "I feel upset and try to stay away from them." (Alex, 13)
- "I feel hurt and insulted. I really treasure relationships with people who treat everyone with respect." (Lila, 13)
- "Angry, small, helpless, frustrated." (Benita, 12)

THE PASSIVE-AGGRESSIVE RESPONSE STYLE

Passive-aggressive people combine the worst attributes of passiveness and aggressiveness. When they feel oppressed, they get their revenge (eventually) in subtle, mean, and sneaky ways.

How can you tell when you're dealing with passive-aggressive people? It's difficult because you're never really sure of how they are feeling...but being with them is often very frustrating. Here are a few examples of passive-aggressive responses:

1

Your dad reminds you that you're supposed to mow the lawn before going out with your friends. You smile and agree to do it. Then you go to the garage and put oil in the gas tank of the lawn mower, destroying the engine.

2

A friend arrives late for a movie. You put on a stony face and give her the silent treatment for the rest of the evening. You resolve to be late for everything you do with her for the next month...and you are.

3

Your teacher makes an error in grading your assignment. You don't say anything about it at the time. After school, you sneak back into the classroom, make sure that your teacher is gone for the day, and super-glue his desk drawers shut.

Passive-aggressive people are basically angry, but they don't know appropriate ways to show their anger. Instead of getting their needs met, they get even. They never let other people know how they really feel.

Having relationships with passive-aggressive people is very difficult. You never know where they stand or how they feel about what's going on, so solving relationship problems is almost impossible. Because of their hidden aggressiveness, you're constantly on guard for the little ways they get back at you for the insults they feel they have endured.

How do young people feel about passive-aggressive people? Here are some of their observations:

- "You can't be honest with them. You never know when they'll come back at you or how." (Tracy, 14)
- "Manipulated and lied to. They say one thing, then do the opposite." (James, 15)
- "You can't trust them." (Marie, 12)
- "I get paranoid." (Bridget, 16)
- "I wish they'd just say what's bothering them, but they never do." (Micah, 17)
- "I think they are totally dishonest, the absolute worst people to be friends with." (Rhonda, 17)
- "They make me crazy." (Pete, 13)

WHAT'S YOUR RESPONSE STYLE?

Your personality has been shaped very gradually over time by the circumstances of your life. It's possible to be totally unaware that some behavior you consider normal is harmful and even self-destructive.

You're probably passive, aggressive, or passive-aggressive at different times with different people. But each of us has a dominant tendency. You may be aware of yours, or you may have to ask someone else what you're like. Finding out is the first step toward learning to be assertive, the best response in all oppressive circumstances.

ASSERTIVENESS: THE ANSWER

Assertiveness allows a person to communicate his or her feelings honestly, directly, and openly when appropriate. It lets you set limits with others about what is and isn't okay with you, and to discuss what you need in order to get along. You can ask for what you want and need without compromising the rights of others. People know who you are, what you think and feel, and what you need to form healthy relationships.

Assertiveness is an important stress-reducing lifeskill. Doing something about oppressive situations relieves a lot of pressure and improves the quality of your life.

Being assertive requires two fundamental competencies:

1. You need to have a clear understanding of your basic rights as a person—rights all people have simply because they are alive.

2. You need to have a range of constructive responses to use when your rights are being abused.

YOUR BASIC RIGHTS

Following are just a few of the basic rights to which all human beings are entitled—including you.

- You have the right to make decisions about your life.
- You have the right to say "no" to the demands of others.
- You have the right to stand up to people who criticize you or put you down.
- You have the right to share your feelings of anger, frustration, confusion, and fear, as well as love and joy.
- You have the right to respond to violations of your rights.

Here are a few more basic rights from *The Gifted Kids Survival Guide (For Ages 11 - 18)* by Judy Galbraith:

- You have a right to attend classes that are interesting and challenging.
- You have a right to do your best work when you want to and less than perfect work when you don't.
- You have a right to be different.
- You have a right to pursue relevant school work at your own speed.

PRACTICING ASSERTIVENESS

Because assertiveness is a skill, you'll need lots of support and practice with different types of assertive responses in order to become proficient. You can use the ASSERT formula to get started in the right direction. This simple formula helps you to remember how to communicate your feelings, exercise your rights, and respond in positive ways when your rights are violated.

The ASSERT Formula

■ The **"A"** stands for "Attention." Before you can work on a problem you're having with another person, you first have to get the person to agree to listen to you. You have to make sure that he or she is ready and willing to hear what you have to say.

■ The first **"S"** stands for "Soon, Simple, Short." Unless you're too upset to be clear about your feelings, try to respond as soon as you realize that your rights have been violated. That way, the circumstances will still be fresh for everyone. State the problem simply and briefly.

■ The second **"S"** stands for "Specific Behavior." Focus on the behavior of the person you're having trouble with. Don't focus on how you feel about the person.

■ The **"E"** stands for "Effect on Me." Help the person to understand the feelings and problems you are experiencing as a result of his or her behavior.

■ The **"R"** stands for "Response." Describe what you need for the relationship to work—the changed behavior that would help you to get along better. Then ask the other person for feedback on your request.

■ The **"T"** stands for "Terms." If all goes well, you should be able to work out an agreement about how to handle similar situations in the future.

Following are two examples of the ASSERT formula in action.

1

The Problem:
*You always have to call your friend
if you want to do something together.
She never calls you.*

Attention: "Juanita, would you be willing to take a few minutes to talk about something that's been bothering me for a long time?"

Soon, Simple, Short: "I feel as if I'm doing all the work in our relationship."

Specific Behavior: "It seems like I'm making all the calls, and I never hear from you."

Effect on Me: "I feel like you don't really care about me, and our friendship isn't that important to you."

Response: "Would you be willing to make more calls to me and plan some of the things we do together?"

Terms: "Thanks. I really appreciate knowing that you care about our relationship and you'll be calling more often."

2

The Problem:
*Your mom is always yelling at you
when you're on the phone
with your friends.*

Attention: "Mom, can we take a second to talk about something that I'm having trouble with?"

Soon, Simple, Short: "I'm having a problem with how you let me know when you want me to get off the phone."

Specific Behavior: "I don't like being yelled at when you feel I've been on the phone too long."

Effect on Me: "When you do that, it embarrasses me in front of my friends."

Response: "Would you be willing to try something different? If you held up two fingers to let me know I have two minutes to get off the phone, that would give me enough time to finish my conversation. It would be easier on both of us."

Terms: "Okay, so you'll hold up two fingers instead of yelling, and I'll get off the phone within two minutes. Thanks for being willing to try this idea."

The ASSERT formula will feel mechanical and awkward at first. Like a baby learning to walk, you won't be able to take natural "steps" for quite awhile. But you will have a place to start. The formula isn't foolproof, it won't always work, and there are some situations in which asserting yourself might make things worse. For example, you don't want to try being assertive with someone who is drunk, violent, or in a rage. You'll have to use good judgment and decide if the other person is able and willing to hear your side of the issue.

For the most part, being assertive reduces stress for everyone involved. Even when the problem is hard to talk about, you're giving the other person a gift just by trying. You're saying, "I'm taking this risk because I care about our relationship and I want it to work."

It's wonderful to express yourself assertively and to see your world change in a way that makes life better for everyone. It gives you a sense of personal power and value. Even if you don't get exactly the response you want, you create the opportunity for other people to meet your needs. Because you express your needs openly and effectively, people know where you stand and what it takes to get along with you. By not being defensive or offensive, you invite direct and honest communication.

Assertive communication reduces the stress associated with things not being right in your world. Expressing your feelings in healthy ways is like having a safety valve that keeps you from reaching the bursting point. Assertiveness is a critical skill for life in the jungle.

"No one can make you feel inferior without your consent."
Eleanor Roosevelt

. . . .

READ MORE ABOUT IT

If you want to know more about assertiveness, read:

Bringing Up Parents: The Teenager's Handbook by Alex J. Packer, Ph.D. (Minneapolis: Free Spirit Publishing, 1992).

Coping Through Assertiveness by Rhoda McFarland (New York: Rosen Publishing Group, 1992).

Stick Up For Yourself! Every Kid's Guide to Personal Power and Positive Self-Esteem by Gershen Kaufman, Ph.D., and Lev Raphael, Ph.D. (Minneapolis: Free Spirit Publishing, 1990).

Your Perfect Right: A Guide to Assertive Living by Robert E. Alberti and Michael L. Emmons (San Luis Obispo, CA: Impact Publishers, Inc., 1990).

. . . .

WEAVING A SAFETY NET

When you're learning to be assertive and take care of #1, you need people around you who will encourage you to try new behaviors and give you permission to make mistakes. Support people are essential when we're trying to change and grow—and when life is especially hard or scary. They can make the difference between getting through and giving in to stress overload. Knowing how to find and form supportive relationships with caring people is a critical lifeskill.

Many people never change their lives for the better, and it's not because they lack the brains or the desire. Instead, they lack the support they need to take the risks required for real change. When we're alone, it's difficult to resist pressure from others to "stay the way you are." We aren't strong enough to fight the force of habit on our own.

To make big changes in our lives, we need others to encourage us and to celebrate our successes—people to be there with and for us when things don't go well, and to hold us accountable to our dream of change when we'd just as soon forget the whole thing.

Supportive relationships help us to deal with fear, frustration, stress, isolation, hopelessness, loneliness, self-destructive behaviors, and other blocks to growing and loving ourselves. Taken together, your support people form a "safety net," much like the net under the tightrope walker at the circus. They help you find the courage to take risks and try new behaviors. When you're out there teetering on your tightrope, it's great to know that there's a group of trustworthy people who care about you and will catch you if you fall.

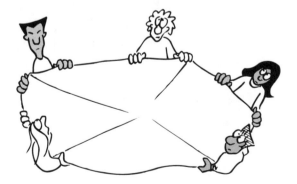

THE CURSE OF
THE PIONEER SPIRIT

As much as we all need a safety net, our culture seems to suggest that we go through life without one. We see this in TV programs and movies, where Rambo and other "super-loners" are tough, brave, and fearless. They seem to have no feelings but anger, and they almost always use violence to solve their problems. Even injured professional football players don't cry after being crunched. They get bandaged and go back to the game.

It's all part of the "pioneer spirit"—the cultural message that tells us to head into the wilderness and handle things on our own. This is the spirit that built a great country full of tough, lonely people, all trying to deal with their daily problems...alone.

Our culture also places a high value on winning—being first, best, and beating others in pursuit of our goals. So we're naturally better at being aggressive and competitive than we are at being supportive. We'd rather stuff our fears and concerns than appear weak or vulnerable in front of the "competition."

As a result of these cultural messages, we end up:

■ putting up a front, looking good, even bending the truth to hide how we really feel and who we really are

■ having friends we don't know very well, and who don't really know us at a deep level

■ never hearing how wonderful, competent, and fascinating we are in spite of our human weaknesses

■ never knowing if we can really trust the people around us for support in a major crisis.

"[We] settle for superficial relationships.
This occurs not only in the case of casual
acquaintances, but even with members of
our own families…. Consequently, we ourselves
do not grow, nor do we help anyone else to
grow. Meanwhile we have to live with
repressed emotions—a dangerous and self-
destructive path to follow."

John Powell, *Why Am I Afraid to Tell You Who I Am?*

BUILDING SUPPORTIVE RELATIONSHIPS

Safety nets don't just happen. The skills necessary to be a supportive person, function in a supportive relationship, and create a safety "net-work" for yourself must be learned and practiced. These skills include the willingness and ability to:

- honestly share what you are thinking and feeling
- listen to someone without being judgmental or critical
- be there when someone really needs you
- offer positive feedback to others to help them see what's right about themselves and the world
- ask for support, objectivity, or feedback from others when you're feeling anxious, vulnerable, or scared.

Taken together, these skills are called *communication*. Honest, open, and direct communication is critical to close relationships. In taking the risk to share what you really think or feel, you allow others to see your true self. This kind of sharing requires trust, and building trust takes time. If you don't have a safety net in place right now, you'll need to start gradually weaving one together. You can't jump in and start sharing yourself without first having a foundation of trust.

First, you'll need to become a supportive person. You'll need to be able to give others the type of support you would like to receive. Then you'll carefully choose your potential support people and slowly begin to build trust relationships.

To understand how this process works, it helps to know the different stages friendships can move through on the way to becoming truly close.

> **"My greatest fear is to go through life without any real friends."**
>
> Holly, 17

THE FIVE LEVELS OF FRIENDSHIP

Think for a moment about the people in your life. Are there some you consider especially close friends? People you know and like who also know and like you? People you call when you have problems or want to go out and do something fun? There are probably some people you think are okay but only spend time with once in awhile. Then there are probably some people you don't talk to unless you have to.

If you had to grade your relationships with the various people you know, you might start by thinking about how much you trust them. This relates directly to how much you'll risk telling them about the hard, painful, or embarrassing parts of your life. A Trust Scale might look like this:

LOW TRUST	MEDIUM TRUST	**HIGH TRUST**
1	**2**	**3**	**4**	**5**

You might want to draw this scale on a piece of paper, then write in the names of the people you know. Where does each person fit on the scale? This will give you a "friendship map" and also indicate what kinds of relationships you need to develop to weave a strong safety net.

One way to assess the degree of trust in a relationship is to consider the things you talk about. What do you share with the other person? What does the other person share with you? You can use this information to organize your relationships into "levels."

■ *Level 1 relationships are about facts.*

"There's a party at Maria's on Saturday night." "We're having a test on Chapter 4 this Friday." "The weather is supposed to be good this weekend." In Level 1 relationships, you share safe, non-threatening, non-personal information—data, facts, knowledge, lessons. The information has little or nothing to do with the person behind the words. A lot of school and class time is spent at Level 1.

■ *Level 2 relationships are about what other people think and say.*

"I hear Debby has a new boyfriend." "They say the new math teacher is really good-looking." "Paulo says the team had a bad time last night." Level 2 is also safe territory, because what is said doesn't come directly from the speaker. In Level 2 exchanges, "you" don't show. No one knows what you think or feel about the information you're sharing because it's something you heard, something you read, or something "they" said. There's no risk of disagreement or rejection. You can't get into trouble because what's being discussed has nothing to do with you.

■ *Level 3 relationships are about what you think.*

"I don't like the color of her hair." "I think that new song is awesome." "I think using drugs is stupid." "I believe we should have a say in how our school is run." Level 3 talk is where risk and trust begin. You start showing yourself to others by revealing your opinions. This is riskier territory, because you let it be known that you stand for something—and you set yourself up for disagreements, being perceived as "different," and possible rejection. At the same time, you give people a sense of who you are and what's important to you.

■ *Level 4 relationships are about feelings.*

You hug someone who is crying about breaking up with a boyfriend. You comfort someone who just slammed his fist into his locker because he had a bad day at school. You're there for someone whose parent just died. In Level 4 relationships, feelings are experienced, shared, and responded to. People don't just talk about being mad, sad, or happy; they express love and joy, lash out, burst into tears, or bounce all over the room. The challenge in Level 4 is to stay present and available in the face of emotional intensity.

It's far more risky to share from the heart than the head, to actually *have* feelings instead of just talking about them. At Level 4, people are very vulnerable. Obviously this requires a lot of trust. You need to feel confident that the people you share yourself with won't make fun of you or go away when you need them the most. This is the level where real connection takes place.

■ *Level 5 relationships are about your feelings for the other person.*

Level 5 is an extension of Level 4, but what you share are the feelings you have for the person you're with. You directly express your love, hurt, anger, frustration, happiness, sadness, shyness, or whatever else is going on between you. These exchanges involve the most disclosure, the greatest risk, and the deepest sharing.

They require a high degree of trust in the other person and in the strength of your relationship.

The hard parts of being at Level 5 involve:

1. knowing what you feel,
2. having the words to express your feelings, and
3. having another person in your life who can tolerate that level of trust.

Level 5 relationships don't just happen. You can't demand them from other people. In most cases, they evolve over time as the trust between you grows. If you spend enough time at a Level 4 relationship and put enough into it, there's a good chance it will move to Level 5.

Here's what happens when we add this new information to our Trust Scale:

LOW TRUST	MEDIUM TRUST	**HIGH TRUST**		
1	**2**	**3**	**4**	**5**
FACTS	THEY SAY	I THINK	I FEEL	I FEEL... ABOUT US

Did you write in the names of the people you know on your original Trust Scale? Based on what you've just learned, would you move any of the names? Are some friends you thought were at Level 5 really at Level 4 or lower? Do you have too many Level 2's or all Level 3's?

Your goal is not to turn all of your relationships into Level 5's. You wouldn't want to be best friends with everyone you know. That would be overwhelming and exhausting. Weaving a strong safety net means that you will want to:

■ develop your understanding and ability to be a 4 or 5 so you can respond to opportunities for more trust when they come along

- have a few 4's and 5's in your life to make up the core elements of your safety net

- also make sure to have lots of 1's, 2's, and 3's around you for the special and important gifts those relationships provide.

It's not necessary to be intense with everyone you meet. People you aren't really close to can still provide you with knowledge, different views of life, and different views of yourself. They can introduce you to new worlds and new challenges.

GIVE AND GET

You may have heard the saying, "What goes around, comes around." That's true for relationships as well. When you make yourself available to others, here's some of what you get in return:

- **You get to know yourself better.** Often it's not until we say something out loud to someone we trust that we know where we really stand. We have many different, sometimes conflicting thoughts and feelings. When we organize them well enough to express them coherently to another person, they become more solid and clear.

- **You develop a larger vocabulary for communicating feelings.** The more you share your feelings, the better you get at recognizing and describing them. Eventually you have a whole new language of emotions, new ways to talk about your complex inner world. Instead of having a vague "uncomfortable sensation" during scary times, you're able to sort out and understand your feelings, describe them to others, and get the help and support you need.

- **You develop close friendships.** When you communicate with others, they communicate with you. Other people start to tell you what they are thinking and feeling. They ask for your perspective on problems they are having, and the trust between you grows.

- **You find out how normal you are.** The more people share themselves with others, the more they discover that everyone has similar fears, problems, and embarrassing moments. You learn that you are more like other people than you ever imagined. When you share yourself with people you trust in mutually supportive relationships, it soon becomes clear that you're a normal human being with normal problems and issues.

If that's not enough, you also get:

- connections with people who validate your self-worth and competency

- the chance to release pent-up stress and avoid stress build-up by sharing your thoughts and feelings with people you trust

- people who will listen to you without judging or criticizing so you can talk freely and safely
- honest feedback about yourself so you can appreciate what's great about you and consider what you might want to change
- nurturing, encouragement, and maybe a hug when you need it
- acceptance and appreciation for who you are
- the security and confidence that comes from trusting and being trusted.

> **"The deepest principle in human nature is the craving to be appreciated."**
> William James

. . . .

READ MORE ABOUT IT

If you want to know more about building supportive relationships and expressing feelings, read:

The Angry Book by Theodore Rubin, M.D. (New York: Macmillan, 1970).

Discovering Self-Expression and Communication by Patricia Kramer (New York: Rosen Publishing Group, 1992).

Everything You Need to Know about Anger by Renor Licata (New York: Rosen Publishing Group, 1992).

The Value of Trust by Rita Milios (New York: Rosen Publishing Group, 1991).

Why Am I Afraid to Tell You Who I Am? by John Powell (New York: Tabor Publishing, 1990).

. . . .

TAKING CHARGE
OF YOUR LIFE

Once your safety net is in place, you're ready to learn the next important lifeskill for managing stress: taking charge of your life. The place to start is by figuring out the "big questions"—like who's steering, and where are you going?

Have you ever felt as if your life is like a ride on a two-seated bike and you're permanently stuck on the back seat? Whenever you try to look ahead, someone blocks your view. You're screaming down the road of life, and all you get to do is pedal.

It's perfectly normal to ask yourself, "Where am I going? Why am I going in this direction? Who decided? What's really important to *me*?" These big questions about your life are very difficult to answer—so difficult that some young people (and lots of adults) choose not to think about them. But not having answers has serious consequences. When you go through life without a sense of direction or purpose and without being in charge, the stress is immense.

You can always let others make your life decisions for you. There are plenty of people who are sure to have ideas about what you should do and who you should be "when you grow up." But when you're following someone else's vision, the only decision you get to make is how hard to pedal and how much energy to invest. It's difficult to maintain enthusiasm and passion for someone else's dream, and sooner or later the journey loses its meaning. What could be an exciting, energizing quest becomes boring, empty work.

Many of the decisions about your life will be made by other people, directly or indirectly. That's the way it is when you're young. Others may determine what school you'll attend, some of the classes you'll take, how late you can stay out, and what household responsibilities will be yours. Some of these decisions may be negotiable, but most will not.

You can probably go along with most of these decisions without sacrificing too much. After all, they represent the "small stuff." The ones you need to worry about are the Big Decisions—those that have to do with who you are becoming and what you will do with your life.

> **"To drift is to be in hell;**
> **to be in heaven is to steer."**
> George Bernard Shaw

THE BIG DECISIONS

It's great to have parents or other caring adults around to help you consider options and provide guidance when you're thinking about where to go with your life. But sometimes adults get carried away and attempt to mold kids into what *they* want them to be.

For example, let's say the whole family loves hockey. Dad played, the Oldest Son practices three nights a week and plays a game every weekend, and Mom is at rinkside for every game. Chances are that poor Junior will be "born with a hockey puck in his mouth." The pressure (subtle and direct) to play hockey will begin while he's still a babe. He'll have this cute baby hockey outfit and miniature hockey things in his crib. There will be posters of hockey players on his walls as he grows up, and the sounds of hockey games ("and he *scoooooooooooores!*") will ring in his ears from the first minute. He may never get the chance to decide for himself if he even *likes* hockey!

THE HOCKEY FAMILY

Big Decisions are often a behind-the-scenes part of your world. Someone else quietly determines who you'll be and invites you to sit on the back of the bike and pedal. You want to do well and please the adults in your life, so you pedal like crazy. Every once in awhile you get rewarded or praised for being such a good pedaler.

If the rewards are sufficient (lots of praise, special privileges, etc.), you may never ask where you're going. Instead, you'll go through your life trying hard to live up to other peoples' expectations, leaving control of your life in their hands.

Letting caring adults have some input into your life choices is a good idea. They have a lot of experience and, deep down, they want what's best for you. Ultimately, though, *it's your life.* Without the sense that you're moving toward a destination that's important *for you,* your life will never have the zest, fire, fun, or passion that comes from having your own dreams and seeing them come true.

> **"My greatest fear is that I will grow up**
> **unhappy and not do any of the things**
> **I want to do."**
>
> Sharon, 16

TAKING CHARGE OF THE BIG DECISIONS

How can you take charge of the Big Decisions in your life? You'll need awareness and special skills. Specifically, you'll need to know:

- that the important choices about your life are yours, and if you can find the courage, you can create a wonderful life for yourself

- how to tell when the Big Decisions are being made for you so you can decide if you want to go along with them or not

- what you value, stand for, believe in, want for yourself, and otherwise consider important elements of the life you are creating

- how to write your own script for the movie called "Your Life"—how to lay out a possible vision for who you can become, then move toward your vision a little every day

- how to get support to take the risks to keep moving toward your vision, especially when the going gets tough.

When other people make Big Decisions for you, they often keep you so busy with smaller decisions that you don't realize what's happening. For example, if you're smart and your family has some money, going to college is often a Big Decision. Instead of being asked *if* you want to go, it will be assumed *that* you want to go. You may get to have some say about where you want to go, what to major in, and whether to live on or off campus—the smaller decisions. Going to college is a great opportunity and may be the best thing for you, but the Big Decision is, "Do I want this for myself at this point in my life?"

On the other hand, if you're not an especially academic person and your family is struggling financially, going to work right after high school can be the Big Decision. You may get to make the smaller decisions, such as where you'll look for a job. Going to work may be the best thing for you, but again, you need to ask yourself, "Is this what I want for myself at this point in my life?" Once a Big Decision has been made—consciously or not, by others or by you—it tends to screen out whole worlds of possible options.

You can plug almost anything into these examples: being musical, being athletic, working in the family business, getting married. Even "not amounting to anything" can be a Big Decision that someone else makes for you—or you make for yourself. Some young people believe it when adults tell them that they're not worth much. When this happens, it's not uncommon to see young people who put a lot of intelligence, creativity, and energy into not looking very good. They become very competent at being incompetent.

The direction a Big Decision takes is important, but it's not the major issue here. It's the *process* of how the decision is made that you need to watch out for. If you're going to pedal—if you're going to put energy into realizing a vision for your life—then you should choose the vision or at least influence it strongly.

There are few things as tragic as a life lived without meaning or for someone else's benefit. True, there is some comfort in not having to face the challenge of making your own Big Decisions. You don't have to take responsibility for your life, and you can blame someone else if it turns out to be boring and uneventful. But these are small satisfactions compared to creating and living a life that's meaningful, exciting, and all yours.

"There are really only two ways to approach
life—as a victim or as a gallant fighter—and
you must decide if you want to act or react,
deal your own cards or play with a stacked
deck. And if you don't decide which way to
play with life, it always plays with you."
Merle Shain

The following exercise can help you discover if any Big
Decisions about your life have already been made for you.

1. List the important goals, choices, beliefs, or directions that
   seem to have been decided about your life. (Remember that
   the absence of goals, or a negative vision about you and
   your future, can also be a Big Decision about your life.)

2. For each item on your list, ask yourself whether it was
   a *conscious* choice on your part. Or has it "always been
   that way"?

3. Make a separate list of the "always-been-that-ways."

4. For each item on this list, try to figure out when the
   decision was made and who made it for you.

You may discover that one person has consistently played the
part of the Big Decider in your life. For most young people, that
person is a parent. You may discover that you haven't had *any*
input into the Big Decisions about your life. Or you may find that
you have been given many opportunities to decide for yourself.
What's important is to be aware that the major choices are ultimately yours, and you can and should be responsible for your life.
When Big Decisions are being made, you need to consciously
decide if you want to agree with them or not.

In discussing Big Decisions with the adults in your life, you
may find it helpful to share the following message with them.

A SPECIAL MESSAGE FOR PARENTS

We support you in wanting the best for your children, and *Fighting Invisible Tigers* has been written with that in mind.

But the pace at which the world is changing practically guarantees that much of your experience and many of the skills you needed for your world will not be relevant to the world your children are facing. Your kids need to hear about your love for them, the values you hold high, your beliefs about how you see the world, and your feelings about what is important. Beyond that, one of the greatest gifts parents can offer their children is encouragement and support to develop their own capacity for personal choice.

The earlier young people start taking responsibility for making choices and accepting the consequences, the sooner they will gain the confidence and wisdom necessary to manage life in *their* jungle.

> **"Children require guidance and sympathy far more than instruction."**
> Anne Sullivan

When young people were asked, "What's the hardest part about getting along with your parents?," here is what some of them said:

■ "They don't give me any freedom. I get good grades and never come home drunk or on drugs. I'm a great kid, but they still don't trust me enough to live my own life." (Joel, 16)

■ "They don't understand my age group." (Elise, 15)

- "They still want me to be their 'little girl.' I don't have enough privacy." (Tracy, 18)
- "They try too hard to be buddy-buddy. I already have a best friend. I just need some parents." (Lila, 13)
- "Making them realize what year we are living in." (Suzanne, 17)
- "They think they know exactly what's going on, but they really don't live in my world." (Jeff, 16)
- "They expect me to act like I'm 25, but I still need them like when I was 10." (Maria, 18)
- "Making them understand that I'm growing up." (Rose, 15)

WRITING YOUR OWN SCRIPT

If you're going to make the Big Decisions in your life, you may need some help getting started. The art of creating a vision for your life is not taught in many places. Often it isn't until your last year of high school that someone will come up to you and ask, "What are you going to do after graduation?" If all you can say is "I don't know" or "Party!," you could be headed for trouble.

Imagine that your life is a movie and you get to write the script. You may not be able to direct every scene, but at least you can decide how the overall plot will unfold.

It takes courage to script your life. When you make choices, you also become responsible for them. (Not making choices is *deciding* not to choose.) If the movie turns out to be a dud, you'll bear the consequences. Then again, it may end up winning the Academy Award for Best Picture. The joy, satisfaction, and self-confidence that come from seeing your dreams and goals become realities are very rewarding.

Writing your life's script involves three basic steps:

1. creating a personal vision of what you want your life to become,
2. bringing the future into the present, and
3. deciding what you can do today to move toward your vision.

CREATING A PERSONAL VISION

For many young people, the plan for their life involves nothing more than getting to school, passing some tests, getting a job, and maybe having some fun—just getting by. Others are more focused. They want to have a lot of friends, learn about specific subjects, get good grades, or make the team. While these goals do make up a personal vision, it's a bit limited in scope. If you're going to dream, why not dream big?

A good place to start is by getting in touch with the values you feel are worth building a life around. Do you believe in the importance of family, a spiritual life, knowledge and education, rock-and-roll, or being a vegetarian? Who are your heroes and heroines, the people you think are incredible and are good role models for your life? Who are the people you've been powerfully impressed by over the years, and what makes them stand out?

As you begin to answer these questions, a composite picture will emerge of a person you might become and a life you might create. Discovering what's really important to *you* and what you want for *yourself* must be the starting place for your personal vision. After that, just add a little imagination.

When young people were asked, "What are the most important things in your life?," here is what they said:

- "My family and friends, my cat and my violin." (Alissa, 15)
- "Myself connected to friends, change, and learning and wisdom." (Ramone, 18)
- "Family, religion, knowledge." (Steve, 17)
- "Family, friends, and future. As my family grows up, they become more important. As I grow up, my friends get closer and more dear. As the future gets closer, it's more exciting." (Suzanne, 17)
- "My relationship with God, guys, and people." (Lila, 13)
- "Baseball, school, and life itself." (Joel, 16)
- "My education, happiness, and a healthy body and mind." (Amy, 15)
- "My best friend, my figure skating, and my time alone, when I can make sure I am still sane and know exactly who I am." (Elizabeth, 16)

Your personal vision can extend beyond the present, beyond tomorrow, and even into the distant future. You can start *now* to craft the life you want to live *someday*. You can always change your vision along the way as you learn more about life and yourself. Visions should be flexible. What kind of life would you like for yourself in your 20's, 30's and 40's...maybe even your 70's and 80's? You decide. It's *your* movie.

In creating your personal vision, don't let *anything*, real or imagined, restrict your thinking. For this activity, there are no limits. Let your imagination run wild. Even the most bizarre-sounding idea may contain the seeds of a possible interest that could become an important part of your life. The world is better at encouraging us to be practical and limited in our thinking than to have grand dreams for ourselves. You'll need to overcome this barrier if you're going to have a wide range of possible choices in your personal vision.

Your vision should include things you've never tried, maybe even things no one has ever tried. A lot of young people are reluctant to leave the security and rewards that come from the things they can do well. There's nothing wrong with doing the things you do best over and over again. But if your focus is too narrow, you'll get in a rut, invite boredom, and become a boring person. You'll never grow the strong self-esteem that comes from trying new things and only occasionally succeeding. Taking the risks to explore areas that aren't easy for us opens us up to new possibilities and capabilities.

"A rut is just a long, skinny grave."
Earl Hipp

When young people were asked, "What are some things you'd really like to try—and what's stopping you?," here is what they said:

- "I'd like to pack up sometime, grab a friend or two, and hit the road for a couple of days." *What's stopping you?* "My parents wouldn't like it, and I don't have a car." (Jerome, 16)

- "I wish I could try a new personality." *What's stopping you?* "A lot of people like the one I have." (Heather, 12)

- "I think about writing a story and sending it to a publisher." *What's stopping you?* "Fear of rejection." (Kelly, 15)

- "I'd like to try scuba diving." *What's stopping you?* "My mom would probably have a heart attack." (Jason, 17)

- "I'm interested in hang gliding." *What's stopping you?* "I'm not old enough for lessons, and I'm scared of heights." (Laura, 14)

- "Anything." *What's stopping you?* "Me." (Kathy, 14)

The following questions are designed to help you meet the challenge of creating a big, broad personal vision. You may want to keep your responses in a special notebook or journal so you can re-visit them on occasion. Remember, there are no wrong answers, and at this point, the more wild and creative you are, the more diverse and interesting your life may become. Both the questions and your responses will change as you learn more about the world and yourself.

- What will I be known for in my later years?

- What hobbies will I develop?

- Will I continue my education? How, and in what form?

- What parts of the planet will I visit?

- What could I invent to become famous?

- What will my community of friends and relations look like?

- Will I marry?

- Will I have children? If so, how many?

- How will I develop my spirituality?

- What will I do to keep myself healthy?

- How will I earn a living?

- In my old age, what will be the three most important things in my life?

You may want to plan to re-visit your vision at regular intervals—every six months, every year, or more often. You can refine your vision as needed to make room for the new, growing you. Over time, it will become a map that will help you find your way to the right life for you.

> **"You may be disappointed if you fail,**
> **but you are doomed if you don't try."**
>
> Beverly Sills

BRINGING THE FUTURE INTO THE PRESENT

Once you have a vision of the future in place, the next step is to bring the future into the present. That way, you can feel as if you're moving toward your dreams a little bit every day.

Your personal vision contains many goals, some stated directly and some implied. For example, if you write, "I will earn my living as an astronaut," that statement includes your ultimate goal and implies many sub-goals leading up to it: learning the requirements for the space program, going to college, getting physically fit, developing a science specialty, applying to the program, etc. In other words, you won't become an astronaut just by creating a vision. You'll need to develop and follow a plan.

It's never too soon to start planning for each of your personal vision goals. Remember that if you don't create your own plan, someone else will do it for you, and you may find yourself pedaling into a life without meaning.

> **"When you have planned well on both long-**
> **term and short-term levels, then goals and**
> **activities fit together like well-meshed gears."**
>
> Alan Lakein, *How to Get Control of*
> *Your Time and Your Life*

123

Developing Your Plan

For each goal in your personal vision, you can develop a mini-plan. Each plan should have the following elements:

- a goal statement
- a list of the steps leading up to your goal, starting with very small actions
- descriptions of some of the roadblocks you might encounter and ideas for getting around them
- a list of some of the resources you can use to achieve your goal
- a description of the ways you will measure your progress toward your goal.

For example, let's assume that one of your personal vision goals is to stay physically fit for life. Here's one version of how your plan might look:

1. GOAL STATEMENT

To stay physically fit for life

2. GOAL DEVELOPMENT STEPS

- make a list of why being physically fit will be good for me and put it somewhere I can see it every day
- make a list of physical activities I might enjoy
- talk to people who are familiar with these activities
- find out what equipment I'd need for each activity and the related costs
- choose one activity I like (or more—variety makes it more interesting)
- set up an easy schedule for starters
- find other people who have the same interest(s) and spend time with them

3. ROADBLOCKS

What might happen:	*What I can do:*
my friends will make fun of me	get support from new people; check out some books on the subject; find an activity partner; learn how to deal assertively with people who make fun of me
the equipment I need will be too expensive	find ways to make extra money; figure out what to do until I can afford good equipment; borrow equipment; get a loan from a parent, relative, or friend
I'll start off with enthusiasm, but my lazy nature and lack of self-discipline will eventually destroy my plans	develop a weekly schedule and put it in a visible place; don't over-challenge myself; plan on some rewards for small successes; have at least two activity partners

4. HELPFUL RESOURCES

- library books on the activity
- ask Juanita about her fitness group
- find out where Chou gets her running shoes
- get information from the President's Council on Physical Fitness
- talk to the Physical Education teacher

5. PROGRESS/SUCCESS CRITERIA

- I am doing my activity three times a week
- I am feeling better physically
- I am piling up the continuous weeks of success
- I have more energy
- my activity partner and I have a normal routine
- I am looking forward to my activity days

It takes time and commitment to go through this process with each of the goals in your personal vision. But unless you make specific plans, your vision will never be more than wishful thinking. Like the donkey that follows a carrot on a stick, you'll be moving through life without ever coming closer to your dreams.

DECIDING WHAT YOU CAN DO TODAY

The final step in writing your life's script is to move toward your vision in some small way every day. You make a plan, keep your goal in mind, and do something to make it a reality, every day.

Taking charge of your life means making plans to do the things that move you toward your dreams. The more you plan, the more options you will face each day. This happy thought can be a nightmare in disguise if you already feel overwhelmed by all the things you have to do.

Many young people report that there is already "too much going on" in their lives and they don't know how they're going to get it all done. Many believe that they have to stay on top of everything. They are experiencing huge amounts of stress because they can't manage it all. They are scrambling every minute and, in the process, have become their own worst tigers.

If you've been growing whiskers and a tail, there is an alternative to turning yourself in at the zoo. It's called *time management*. It can help you sort through your goals, plans, and all the other things you have to do each day. Time management helps you decide what's really important *today* and which activities you should attend to first. It ensures that you keep the long-term goals of your personal vision in mind while doing your homework and taking out the garbage.

"Without discipline, there's no life at all."
Katharine Hepburn

Time Management

The key to time management is prioritizing your activities. There are many different ways to approach this challenge, and any one of them will help you to feel less driven and stressed. One system is called the "ABC" method. Here's how it works:

1. **Make a "things-to-do" list. As part of this process, go to your personal vision goals and choose two or three activities from each that you could do today.**

   Here's an example:

   Do something fun with my friends
   Write a letter to Aunt Erma
   Go to the library for information on the astronaut program
   Write paper for Friday's history class
   Shop for running shoes
   Get sister's birthday present
   Buy a bus pass
   Listen to relaxation tape
   Go to library to start researching English paper due next week
   Go for a 1/2-mile walk with Ann
   Call for the job interview

2. **Rank each item on your list according to this scale: A (for Very Important, Must Be Done), B (for Kind of Important, Can Wait) and C (for Nice to Do, but Not Essential).**

   Let's say that one of your most important goals is to decrease the amount of stress in your life. As a result, regular relaxation is a high-priority item for you. You want to make time for it, not find time for it after everything else is done. Given these priorities, "do something fun with my friends" and "listen to relaxation tapes" will both be A's.

You also have two papers due soon: a history paper for this Friday, and an English paper for next week. Obviously the history paper will take precedence. You'll give it an A, and your up-front work for your English paper will get a B.

When you get done, your list looks something like this:

A Do something fun with my friends
C Write a letter to Aunt Erma
C Go to the library for information on the astronaut program
A Write paper for Friday's history class
C Shop for running shoes
B Get sister's birthday present
A Buy a bus pass
A Listen to relaxation tape
B Go to library to start researching English paper due next week
B Go for a 1/2-mile walk with Ann
A Call for the job interview

3. Rank all of your A's, B's, and C's individually (since you have several of each). The most important A should be given an A-1 ranking; the next most important, A-2; and so on through your list.

Here's what your list looks like now:

A-1 Write paper for Friday's history class
A-2 Call for the job interview
A-3 Buy a bus pass
A-4 Listen to relaxation tape
A-5 Do something fun with my friends
B-1 Go for a 1/2-mile walk with Ann
B-2 Get sister's birthday present
B-3 Go to library to start researching English paper due next week
C-1 Shop for running shoes
C-2 Write a letter to Aunt Erma
C-3 Go to the library for information on the astronaut program

At this point, you know which items are top priority and which can wait. You can start attacking them methodically and relax in the comfort of knowing the important things are getting done on time. When you finish with the A's, step right into the B's.

This approach might seem complicated at first, but it goes very quickly once you have tried it a few times. When you start reaping some of the benefits of managing your time, you'll want to become a master.

Two tips to keep in mind along the way:

- Your goal is *not* to accomplish everything on your list. If that's how things work out, great, but don't push it. Just do the best you can in the time you've got. At least you'll be getting the important things done.

- Don't treat your list as if it's carved in stone. Your priorities will change from one day to the next, and sometimes from one hour to the next. For example, you learn that the due date on your history paper has been pushed back a week. Or your friend Ann can't go for a walk until tomorrow. Stay flexible.

Making a things-to-do list gives you a sense of direction. But unless you rank the items on your list, you're left with an assortment of "got-to-dos," all of which seem to want to be done first. You fall into a "do-everything-now-or-else" mentality, which almost guarantees that every day will be full of stress and panic. In all the confusion, you risk not doing anything that's really important to your personal vision. You wind up pedaling like crazy without going anywhere meaningful.

When you manage your time, you do something every day that relates to your goals. This reduces stress and creates a sense of accomplishment. Even a small step brings you closer to the person you want to become.

"Time is life. It is irreversible and irreplaceable. To waste your time is to waste your life, but to master your time is to master your life and make the most of it."

Alan Lakein, *How to Get Control of Your Time and Your Life*

. . . .

READ MORE ABOUT IT

If you want to know more about time management, read:

Discovering Personal Goals by Patrica Kramer (New York: Rosen Publishing Group, 1991.)

Getting Things Done by Edwin C. Bliss (New York: Bantam Books, 1984.)

How to Get Control of Your Time and Your Life, by Alan Lakein (New York: NAL Dutton, 1989.)

. . . .

A SHORT COURSE IN RISK-TAKING

Which would you rather do?

- Hang out with your friends at the mall, or go to a party where you won't know anyone?
- Spend the weekend studying a little and watching the tube a lot, or plan and then take a canoe trip with new friends?
- Go to school and just get by, or try to do well in a class you need to take if you plan to be an astronaut?

In each of these situations, the second option means taking a risk. Many of the changes described in this book also may mean taking risks to behave or operate differently.

Taking a risk can be like going on a dangerous journey. You don't know what you'll encounter along the way, and your current level of knowledge and experience may not be enough to see you through. A real learning adventure, by definition, means that you have to learn new things in order to succeed. You have to grow to get through it. Taking risks can be scary.

When people start to think about going on learning adventures that are a little (or a lot) risky, they often encounter two dangerous critters that can end the adventure before it begins. The "Whatif" and "Wouldbut" are naturally attracted to people who are thinking about taking the risks to learn and grow. How can you tell if you've been bitten by these creatures? You'll find yourself saying things like, "I could do that, but *what if*...." or "I *would* do that, *but*...." People who have serious Whatif/Wouldbut bites almost always choose not to risk, not to grow or change, and to just hide out.

Because all learning and personal growth means taking some risks, you'll need some special risk-taking skills to successfully fight off the Whatif and Wouldbut. The following tips should help you find the courage to begin your learning adventure in spite of any anxiety you may feel.

START SMALL

Don't focus on the end of your journey, but on the next step you can take. Maybe your personal vision includes running a marathon someday. Most marathons are approximately 26 miles, a distance that might seem impossible to you today. It wouldn't make much sense to enter your first marathon and just start running. But people all over the world train for marathons by running short distances, then longer ones. On the day of the race, they run one mile at a time.

For you, starting small might mean going to the library and getting a book on fitness running, or talking to someone who has completed a marathon. The risk at this level is very low. As your understanding of the challenge grows, you become willing to take the next step...and the next...and the next until you're crossing the finish line.

GIVE YOURSELF PERMISSION TO BE AVERAGE OR WORSE

This can be tough if you're the kind of person who wants to do a great job at everything you try. If you're starting something that's totally new to you, you probably won't be good at it for quite awhile. Be kind to yourself and give yourself permission to learn. Expect to feel incompetent with your new endeavor, at least for a time. See if you can focus on the excitement of learning and the positive feeling that you're growing in new directions. On any learning adventure, it's important to view your "failures" as necessary stops on the way to acquiring new knowledge or skills.

> **"It's okay if you mess up.**
> **You should give yourself a break."**
>
> Billy Joel

GET SUPPORT

No one should go on a risky adventure alone. Find four or five people who will give you help and encouragement. Meet with them regularly and invite their support, comments, and constructive feedback.

You may want people who have special knowledge or skills; perhaps they have been where your learning adventure is headed. Or it may be enough to have a few friends around to remind you that you're lovable and capable even if you're not progressing as fast as you would like.

There will be times when your enthusiasm weakens or you get hopeless and feel like quitting. Everyone has moments like these; they are a predictable part of learning and growing. Caring, understanding friends can help you find the strength to go on.

CELEBRATE YOURSELF

Rejoice at any success, no matter how insignificant it may seem. Remember that big changes don't just happen. Instead, they are the result of consistently meeting small goals over and over again.

Any little step is progress and deserves to be celebrated. Design a reward system for yourself. At certain mileposts on your adventure, plan for treats, gifts—even parties.

READ MORE ABOUT IT

If you want to know more about risk-taking, read:

Discovering Self-Confidence by Patricia Kramer (New York: Rosen Publishing Group, 1991).

Feel the Fear and Do It Anyway by Susan Jeffers, Ph.D. (New York: Fawcett Columbine, 1988).

THE BURDEN OF PERFECTIONISM

As you journey through your challenging life, you can make choices that will dramatically increase or decrease the stress you experience. One of these choices has to do with how you see yourself.

Are you always wondering if what you do is good enough...if who you are is good enough? If so, you may be struggling with the burden of perfectionism. The main problem with being a perfectionist is that your self-esteem is on the line every minute.

Perfectionists can't enjoy an activity unless they are outstanding at it. If they are a notch or two less than outstanding, their ego takes a dive. In fact, perfectionism is a huge barrier to growing and changing because it keeps people locked into doing only those things they can do well. Taken to the extreme, perfectionism can prevent you from even trying anything new. It can severely limit the development of your personal vision and make you a bored (and boring) individual.

> **"When you aim for perfection,
> you discover it's a moving target."**
> George Fisher

ARE YOU A PERFECTIONIST?

You may have to get objective feedback from others to realize how badly you are afflicted. (We're all a little perfectionistic at times.) Meanwhile, here's a self-assessment that can make you more aware of your own perfectionist tendencies.

Read each statement and decide how much you agree with it. Use the following numbers. Write the numbers on a separate sheet of paper. You'll be adding them up at the end.

- + 2 = I agree very much
- + 1 = I agree somewhat
- 0 = I feel neutral about this
- -1 = I disagree slightly
- -2 = I disagree strongly

1. If I don't set the highest standards for myself, I am likely to end up a second-rate person.
2. People will think less of me if I make mistakes.
3. If I can't do something really well, there's little point in doing it at all.
4. I should be upset if I make a mistake.
5. If I try hard enough, I should be able to excel at anything I attempt to do.
6. It's immature to display any weakness or childlike behaviors.

7. I shouldn't have to repeat the same mistake more than once.

8. An average performance is bound to be unsatisfying to me.

9. Failing at something important makes me less of a person.

10. If I scold myself for failing to live up to my expectations, it will help me to do better the next time.

Now total your score. Plus and minus numbers cancel each other out. An above-zero score indicates a tendency toward perfectionism. A below-zero score signifies a less perfectionist mindset.

RELIEF FROM THE BURDEN

What did you learn from the self-assessment? If you scored above zero, you may want to consider doing some things differently. Here are some suggestions for starters:

- Decide how much time you're going to spend on a given project and stick to it. For a perfectionist, no amount of effort is ever enough. Practice saying, "It's time to stop. I've done a good job, and now I'll go on to something else."

- Reward yourself for just being in the process of learning something new, regardless of how well you are doing.

- Redefine the words "failure" and "mistake" in your mind. Instead of letting them stand for being inadequate or a total failure at life, see them as proof that you are learning and growing.

- Ask friends, a parent, and/or a counselor—people you trust—to give you objective feedback on your efforts. They may be able to offer insights into "reasonable" responses to specific challenges.

- Go to the library and get a book on perfectionism. A lot has been written about it because it's a problem for so many people.

Perfectionism is a guaranteed prescription for feeling bad about yourself. Trying to be perfect is the quickest path to feeling like a failure because being perfect is impossible. Relief from the burden of perfectionism—and the stress it creates—will feel wonderful, and you'll discover that it's much more interesting and fun to just be a normal human being.

> **"I've learned that nobody's perfect, and I don't expect myself to be perfect anymore."**
> Carly Simon

. . . .

READ MORE ABOUT IT

If you want to know more about perfectionism, read:

Coping with Academic Anxiety by Allen J. Ottens, Ph.D. (New York: Rosen Publishing Group, 1991).

Coping with Family Expectations by Margaret Hill (New York: Rosen Publishing Group, 1990).

Coping with Your Inner Critic by Matthew Ignoffo, Ph.D. (New York: Rosen Publishing Group, 1990).

Feeling Good: The New Mood Therapy by David Burns (New York: Avon Books, 1992).

Perfectionism: What's Bad about Being Too Good? by Miriam Adderholdt-Elliott, Ph.D. (Minneapolis: Free Spirit Publishing, 1987).

. . . .

GROWING
A FUNNY BONE

There is yet another choice you can make that will greatly reduce the stress you feel on your life journey. You can choose to see the lighter side of things. In other words, be sure to bring your sense of humor.

As you get better at managing the stress in your life, weaving a safety net of friends, and moving toward your personal vision, you'll feel better about yourself and your life. You'll naturally feel lighter, happier, and more like laughing.

There is a physiological reason for this: As stress decreases, your funny bone starts to grow. You probably didn't know that. You may not even believe that you have a funny bone. And you thought you knew the human body!

A funny bone can help to keep things in perspective when life is being particularly confusing or nasty. A sense of humor, frequent laughter, and solid play time are essential to a healthy sense of yourself. Being able to see the humor in difficult situations, and to laugh at yourself on a regular basis, also makes you a person who is more fun to be around.

A sense of humor can help to keep you physically healthy. Ever since 1980, when a man named Norman Cousins cured himself of a terminal disease by watching funny films, scientists have been studying the health effects of having a sense of humor.

According to Dr. William Fry of Stanford University, laughter increases one's respiratory activity (breathing rate), oxygen exchange, muscular activity, and heart rate. It stimulates the cardiovascular system, the sympathetic nervous system, and the pituitary gland and leads to an overall positive biochemical state. Dr. Fry further points out:

"In the ordinary course of human events, humor protects us from the destructive influences of negative emotions."

What does this mean for you? When you laugh, you feel better and happier. The better and happier you feel, the more you laugh, and the bigger your funny bone gets. Around and around it goes in a big *positive* circle. Life should be about having fun!

> **"Seven days without laughter makes
> one weak."**
>
> Dr. Joel Goodman

These concepts are not new. Some 80 years ago, a man named Bernarr MacFadden (one of the first psychophysiologists) extolled the virtues of laughter. In his book, *Vitality Supreme,* he noted that one way to avoid "tragical consequences" (an old-fashioned way of saying "a lot of stress") was to find some way of "arousing the emotions expressed in a good hearty laugh." He went on to say:

> *"There is no question that laughter has valuable vitalizing qualities. It undoubtedly adds to one's stamina. It gives one a hopeful spirit. It leads one to look upon the bright side of life. When you can laugh, the sun is shining regardless of how many clouds obscure the sky."*

Laughing can sometimes be difficult for those of us who are a little shy and self-conscious. Like the other skills described in *Fighting Invisible Tigers*, this valuable stress-reducer can be learned and practiced. MacFadden offered the following instructions on how to laugh for you to try:

> *"First of all assume a laughing position, in order to laugh properly and to secure the best results. Stand with the feet far apart, and with the knees slightly bent. Now bring the palms of the hands down and 'slap' them vigorously on the legs just above the knees, and then swing your bent arms overhead, making a noise as nearly as possible like laughing. Yes, you are quite right, it will sound very much like a cold stage laugh at first, and you will have to force it, but as you go on with the experiment it will gradually become more natural. Continue this long enough and I defy anyone to differentiate the emotions aroused from those associated with a real, spontaneous laugh."*

Developing a huge funny bone (and a great laugh) will also make the world a better place. In his book, *J'ARM for the Health of It,* Dr. Dale Anderson observes that just by smiling, you can start a "happy-demic" by spreading humor and a positive attitude. He believes that:

> *"...smiles, like laughs, are contagious, prompting the saying, 'Grin and share it'...the day goes the way the corners of the mouth go. We can, by putting a smile on our face, get better 'smileage' out of life. It's more important what you wear on your face than what you wear head to toe. I sum it up by saying that smiling is a free way to increase your 'face value.'"*

"Strange, when you come to think of it, that of all the countless folk who have lived before our time on this planet not one is known in history or in legend as having died of laughter."

Max Beerbohm

EIGHT WAYS TO GROW YOUR FUNNY BONE

If you're stressed-out or too serious too much of the time, try these tips for growing a funny bone:

1. Find funny people to hang out with—people with a good sense of humor who make you laugh. Make them part of your safety net.

2. Go to funny movies often. If you have a choice between laughing, seeing something serious, or scaring the daylights out of yourself, try to see films that make you laugh.

3. Watch funny TV or rent funny videos. There are programs that specialize in stand-up comedians, old slapstick films, and off-the-wall, weird material.

4. If at all possible, go to see live comedy. Stand-up comedians are specialists in seeing the lighter side of life. They know how to find humor everywhere.

5. Read humorous authors, cartoon books, or the comics in the Sunday paper. Cut out great cartoons and tape them in your locker or inside the cover of a notebook.

6. Listen to comedy recordings.

7. Learn a joke a week and share it with everyone you know (even if you get groans in return). This will help others to see you as a person with a lighter side.

8. Laugh whenever and wherever you get the chance.

READ MORE ABOUT IT

If you want to know more about humor and health, read:

Anatomy of an Illness as Perceived by the Patient by Norman Cousins (New York: Bantam Books, 1983).

Laugh after Laugh: The Healing Power of Humor by Raymond Moody (Jacksonville, FL: Headwaters Press, 1978).

The Laughter Prescription by L. Peter and B. Dana (New York: Ballantine Books, 1988).

AFTERWORD: NOW WHAT?

I hope that this look at the subject of stress and what you can do about it has made the "jungle" of your life more understandable and a little less threatening. I also hope that you have a larger sense of your own power to influence the direction your life takes, and that this book has helped you to develop a positive personal vision.

Imagine a life that includes:

- the ability to recognize when you're at your limits and know what to do to take great care of yourself
- better physical health, times of quiet and deep rest, and the best foods that are available to you
- lots of good friends and a number of "best friends"
- the ability to assertively communicate your needs and feelings
- the ability to recognize and resist manipulation and Big Decisions by others
- a strong sense of personal direction

- the ability to organize and prioritize your life to make sure the important things get done
- diversity and variety in your activities
- a willingness to take the risks necessary to grow and learn
- the ability to accept the responsibility and challenge of shaping your life into an experience that is richly meaningful and exciting for you
- the ability to have lots of fun and feel enormous satisfaction with how your life is unfolding.

Is this scenario idealistic? Maybe, maybe not. Much of it is up to you. Unfortunately, you may run up against some barriers. You may decide that you want to change, but the world won't always be on your side. Training and support for many of the important lifeskills described here still aren't readily available in many schools. (If you do have access to them, you are very lucky, and you should go thank someone.) Strangely, it's often only *after* young people have reached the limits of their coping ability and have chosen destructive behaviors to deal with stress that they are given skill-building and support group activities—for "rehabilitation"!

Young people are often given subtle messages to adapt to and accept "the system." If you have problems adapting, the implication is that *you're* the problem, not the system. Schools are struggling with change and trying to become more effective at preparing young people for their own futures. But it may be some time before they do their part to teach young people all the skills necessary for becoming competent, successful adults. In the meantime, you may not get much help in acquiring new lifeskills. You might even face a great deal of resistance if you push the system to meet your needs.

By reading this book, you have taken a valuable first step toward acquiring the tools to manage the stressors you will encounter. You have a bigger picture of how you might design the life you want—and an understanding of the skills you'll need to make it happen. My hope is that your intelligence, good instincts, self-respect, and healthy drive will keep you moving in the direction that's best for you.

Here are some last-minute reminders to speed you along:

- Have the courage to dream big dreams. You're worth it.

- Get the support you need to take the important risks and to move toward your dreams. Wishing instead of acting leads to a life of regrets.

- Be very serious about *your* needs and *your* agenda. It's important to remain open to the experience and wisdom of adults you trust; after all, you're still learning about life. But your needs and views do count. It's never too soon to learn to assert yourself in constructive ways.

- Find people who will support you. A strong safety net may be the most important resource of all. We are all in this life alone...together.

- Find good role models—people you respect—and learn from them. We all need heroes and heroines.

- Write to me and tell me how you're doing and what you're learning. I may be able to help others by sharing your story in my books and talks. You can write to me at this address:

> Earl Hipp
> c/o Free Spirit Publishing Inc.
> 400 First Avenue North, Suite 616
> Minneapolis, MN 55401-1730

Finally, *never give up on yourself.* You are a miracle of the universe. You deserve the best in self-care and self-love. Go for it!

> **"I want you to get excited about who you are, what you are, what you have, and what can still be for you. I want to inspire you to see that you can go far beyond where you are right now."**
> Virginia Satir, *Peoplemaking*

INDEX

ABOUT THE AUTHOR

Earl Hipp is a speaker, trainer, consultant, author, and president of Human Resource Development, Inc., a company that helps employees understand and grow through the almost constant changes in today's workplace. He has a B.A. in Psychology and a Master's Degree in Psychophysiology. For four years, he was a clinical psychologist at a Minneapolis H.M.O., where he helped hundreds of people to better understand, cope with, and grow from the changes in their lives.

Earl is a member of the National Speakers Association and is listed in *Who's Who in Professional Speaking.* He is available to speak to groups on the topics of his books. You can reach him by writing to:

Earl Hipp
c/o Free Spirit Publishing Inc.
217 Fifth Avenue North, Suite 200
Minneapolis, MN 55401-1299

Other Great Books from Free Spirit

What Teens Need To Succeed
Proven, Practical Ways To Shape Your Own Future
by Peter L. Benson, Ph.D., Judy Galbraith, M.A., and Pamela Espeland
Based on a nationwide survey, this book describes 40 developmental "assets" all teens need to succeed in life, then gives hundreds of suggestions teens can use to build their own assets wherever they are. For ages 11 & up.
$14.95; 368 pp.; softcover; illus.; 7¼" x 9¼"

Bringing Up Parents
The Teenager's Handbook
by Alex J. Packer, Ph.D.
Straight talk and specific suggestions on how teens can resolve conflict with parents, improve family relationships, earn trust, and accept responsibility. Written with wisdom and humor, this book emphasizes open communication, mutual respect, and common sense. For ages 13 & up.
$14.95; 272 pp.; softcover; illus.; 7¼" x 9¼"

Kids With Courage
True Stories About Young People Making a Difference
by Barbara A. Lewis
Eighteen remarkable kids speak out, fight back, come to the rescue, and stand up for their beliefs. These true stories prove that anyone, at any age, in any life circumstance, can make a real difference in the world. For ages 11 & up.
$11.95; 184 pp.; softcover; B&W photos; 6" x 9"

Perfectionism
What's Bad About Being Too Good?
Revised and Updated Edition
by Miriam Adderholdt, Ph.D., and Jan Goldberg
This revised and updated edition includes new research and statistics on the causes and consequences of perfectionism, biographical sketches of famous perfectionists and risk takers, and resources for readers that want to know more. For ages 13 & up.
$12.95; 136 pp.; softcover; illus.; 6" x 9"

To place an order or to request a free catalog of
SELF-HELP FOR KIDS® *and* SELF-HELP FOR TEENS® *materials,*
please write, call, email, or visit our Web site:

Free Spirit Publishing Inc.
217 Fifth Avenue North • Suite 200 • Minneapolis, MN 55401-1299
toll-free 800.735.7323 • local 612.338.2068 • fax 612.337.5050
help4kids@freespirit.com • www.freespirit.com